AUTOBIOGRAPHY OF A NON-YOGI

BOOKS BY AMITAVA DASGUPTA

Autobiography of a Non-Yogi: A Scientist's Journey From Hinduism to Christianity (with Lochlainn Seabrook)
Clinical Chemistry, Immunology and Laboratory Quality Control: A Comprehensive Review for Board Preparation, Certification and Clinical Practice
A Health Educator's Guide to Understanding Drugs of Abuse Testing
The Science of Drinking: How Alcohol Affects Your Body and Mind
Accurate Results in the Clinical Laboratory: A Guide to Error Detection and Correction
Beating Drug Tests and Defending Positive Results: A Toxicologist's Perspective
Pharmacogenomics in Clinical Therapeutics
Prescription or Poison?: The Benefits and Dangers of Herbal Remedies
Antioxidants in Food, Vitamins and Supplements: Prevention and Treatment of Disease
Handbook of Drug Monitoring Methods: Therapeutics and Drugs of Abuse
Critical Issues in Alcohol and Drugs of Abuse Testing
Advances in Chromatographic Techniques for Therapeutic Drug Monitoring
Resolving Erroneous Reports in Toxicology and Therapeutic Drug Monitoring: A Comprehensive Guide
Therapeutic Drug Monitoring: Newer Drugs and Biomarkers
Herbal Supplements: Efficacy, Toxicity, Interactions with Western Drugs, and Effects on Clinical Laboratory Tests
Pocket Antioxidants
Alcohol and Its Biomarkers: Clinical Aspects and Laboratory Determination
Pharmacogenomics of Alcohol and Drugs of Abuse
Effects of Herbal Supplements on Clinical Laboratory Test Results
Hematology and Coagulation: A Comprehensive Review for Board Preparation, Certification and Clinical Practice (with Amer Wahed)

BOOKS BY LOCHLAINN SEABROOK

Christ Is All and In All: Rediscovering Your Divine Nature and the Kingdom Within
Jesus and the Gospel of Q: Christ's Pre-Christian Teachings As Recorded in the New Testament
Seabrook's Bible Dictionary of Traditional and Mystical Christian Doctrines
The Way of Holiness: The Story of Religion and Myth From the Cave Bear Cult to Christianity
Christmas Before Christianity: How the Birthday of the "Sun" Became the Birthday of the "Son"
The Secret Jesus: What Your Church Never Taught You About the Christian Savior
The Secret New Testament: What Your Church Never Taught You About Christianity's Holiest Books
The Bible and the Law of Attraction: 99 Teachings of Jesus, the Apostles, and the Prophets
Jesus and the Law of Attraction: The Bible-Based Guide to Creating Perfect Health, Wealth, and Happiness Following Christ's Simple Formula
Britannia Rules: Goddess-Worship in Ancient Anglo-Celtic Society - An Academic Look at the United Kingdom's Matricentric Spiritual Past
The Book of Kelle: An Introduction to Goddess-Worship and the Great Celtic Mother-Goddess Kelle, Original Blessed Lady of Ireland
The Goddess Dictionary of Words and Phrases: Introducing a New Core Vocabulary for the Women's Spirituality Movement
Everything You Were Taught About the Civil War is Wrong, Ask a Southerner!
Everything You Were Taught About American Slavery is Wrong, Ask a Southerner!
Honest Jeff and Dishonest Abe: A Southern Children's Guide to the Civil War
Confederacy 101: Amazing Facts You Never Knew About America's Oldest Political Tradition
The Great Yankee Coverup: What the North Doesn't Want You to Know About Lincoln's War!
Confederate Blood and Treasure: An Interview With Lochlainn Seabrook
Confederate Flag Facts: What Every American Should Know About Dixie's Southern Cross
Princess Diana: Modern Day Moon-Goddess - A Psychoanalytical and Mythological Look at Diana Spencer's Life, Marriage, and Death (with Dr. Jane Goldberg)

AUTOBIOGRAPHY
OF A
NON-YOGI

a scientist's journey from hinduism to christianity

Amitava Dasgupta, Ph.D.

with Lochlainn Seabrook

ILLUSTRATED

Sea Raven Press, Nashville, Tennessee, USA

AUTOBIOGRAPHY OF A NON-YOGI

Published by
Sea Raven Press, Cassidy Ravensdale, President
PO Box 1484, Spring Hill, Tennessee 37174-1484 USA
SeaRavenPress.com • searavenpress@gmail.com

Copyright © 2015 Amitava Dasgupta
in accordance with U.S. and international copyright laws and regulations, as stated and protected under the Berne Union for the Protection of Literary and Artistic Property (Berne Convention), and the Universal Copyright Convention (the UCC). All rights reserved under the Pan-American and International Copyright Conventions.

First Sea Raven Press paperback edition: November 2015
ISBN: 978-1-943737-08-6
Library of Congress Control Number: 2015955736

This work is the copyrighted intellectual property of Amitava Dasgupta and has been registered with the Copyright Office at the Library of Congress in Washington, D.C., USA. No part of this work (including text, covers, drawings, photos, illustrations, maps, images, diagrams, etc.), in whole or in part, may be used, reproduced, stored in a retrieval system, or transmitted, in any form or by any means now known or hereafter invented, without written permission from the publisher. The sale, duplication, hire, lending, copying, digitalization, or reproduction of this material, in any manner or form whatsoever, is also prohibited, and is a violation of federal, civil, and digital copyright law, which provides severe civil and criminal penalties for any violations.

Autobiography of a Non-Yogi: A Scientist's Journey From Hinduism to Christianity, by Amitava Dasgupta, with Lochlainn Seabrook. Includes reference notes.

Front and back cover design and graphic art, book design, layout, and interior art by Lochlainn Seabrook. All images, graphic design, graphic art, font work, and illustrations copyright © Lochlainn Seabrook. Cover design copyright © Lochlainn Seabrook.

The paper used in this book is acid-free and lignin-free. It has been certified by the Sustainable Forestry Initiative and the Forest Stewardship Council and meets all ANSI standards for archival quality paper.

PRINTED & MANUFACTURED IN OCCUPIED TENNESSEE, FORMER CONFEDERATE STATES OF AMERICA

DEDICATION

To my Indian and American Spiritual Teachers.

EPIGRAPH

"The book one must read to learn chemistry is the book of nature. The book from which to learn religion is your own mind and heart. The sage is often ignorant of physical science, because he reads the wrong book—the book within; and the scientist is too often ignorant of religion, because he too reads the wrong book—the book without."

Swami Vivekananda

CONTENTS

A Note to the Reader - 8
Preface, by Amitava Dasgupta - 9

1 WHY I AM A FALLEN HINDU - 13

2 A RELIGIOUS MOTHER & AN ATHEIST FATHER - 44

3 LIFE IN THE UNITED STATES OF AMERICA - 62

4 FROM HINDU SKEPTIC TO CHRISTIAN BELIEVER - 86

5 A GLIMPSE OF HEAVEN: NEAR DEATH EXPERIENCES - 98

6 THE SOUL IS IMMORTAL: PAST LIFE MEMORIES - 127

7 FINDING GOD - 154

Meet the Author, Amitava Dasgupta - 192
Meet the Coauthor, Lochlainn Seabrook - 193

A NOTE TO THE READER

I used several books written in Bengali, an Indian language and the official language of Bangladesh, for much of the information presented in this book. I did not cite these works because English speaking readers will not be able to read them, and also because these books are not available in the U.S. I have used these books for some of the information presented in other chapters, especially Chapter 7.

Amitava Dasgupta

A SPECIAL NOTE FROM THE COAUTHOR
I want to personally thank Dr. Dasgupta for allowing me to be a part of the writing of his autobiography. It has been a true privilege and one of the great honors of my life.

Lochlainn Seabrook

PREFACE

The main purpose of human life is to reunite with God and only God loves us unconditionally. For a person with a strong faith like my wife, my mother, and my in-laws, life is simple and enjoyable. My mother prays to Lord Shiva every day and she strongly believes death is a spiritual rebirth when she will go back to heaven. My wife is a Christian and she attends church almost every Sunday. She has a powerful belief in Jesus and the teachings of the Bible. My mother and my wife get along wonderfully because they both believe in God, although they pray differently.

I am not so fortunate. My father, who passed away in July 2011, was an atheist and he taught me logic from my early adolescent years. He told me that God could not do my homework or help me find a job. Therefore, it would be more helpful for me to study before finals rather than going to temple and praying. He also taught me to be ethical and sympathetic to people who are less fortunate than us.

As Dr. Dasgupta discusses, science and religion meet at the edges of quantum mechanics.

As a teenager I was also influenced by Professor Banerjee, my neighbor and a religious study scholar. He had a magnetic personality and taught me Sanskrit and then Hindu religious texts, such as the Bhagavad Gita, as well as Indian philosophy, including the dialectical materialism first proposed by Charback. Charback's philosophy and writings are similar to the philosophy of Karl Marx and Friedrich Engels.

As a practicing toxicologist and a professor of pathology at a medical school, for many years I was a skeptic, although my spiritual teacher Deepak Babu had a strong influence on me and tried his best to convince me that God exists. Yet I am a fallen Hindu because I love eating beef, do not show respect to Brahmins, and go to the temple only to make my mother happy. I had always looked at religion from a logical point of view, and was convinced that man created God—until June 2011, when my mother returned from the brink of death after my Christian wife prayed at her bedside.

Mother was in a coma and we were ready to withdraw her life support because she had less than a 1% chance of survival, according to medical science. However, she came back to us and, surprisingly, had a vivid vision during her coma in which she saw my wife Alice with two angels. Her life threatening illness did not affect her memory nor her intellectual ability. For me her survival was a miracle and proof of the existence of God. The event transformed my life and I started looking for God using my heart, remembering the teachings of my spiritual teachers in India and seeking knowledge from my American spiritual teachers.

God appears to those who open their hearts and minds and "become as little children."

This book tells about my life journey from being a longtime skeptic—despite meeting gifted spiritual teachers in India and the U.S.—to a believer. My wife's faith also influenced me, but my mother's return from death was an eye opening experience that altered my worldview. God showed me proof of his existence by granting my wife's prayer. I have studied the Hindu religion for many years. But I also have a keen interest in the Bible and scholarly books on Christianity. In a sense then, this book is my odyssey from Brahma to Jehovah.

I was contemplating writing this book for a while, when we discovered Sea Raven Press, a well respected independent publisher of religious and history titles. The owner, Cassidy Ravensdale, kindly agreed to publish my manuscript. Without her help this book would never have seen the light of day. I also want to thank award-winning author and esteemed historian Lochlainn Seabrook for his many outstanding additions to the manuscript, as well as for his ideas, editing skills, and captioned illustrations. He came up with the title and helped shape many of my words into their present form, hence his name appears on the cover.

I wrote this book using both my head and my heart. In Chapter 1, I discuss various theories explaining the origin of religion, as well as how the human brain is wired to experience religious/spiritual bliss. Chapters 2 and 3 entail my explorations of skepticism, and in Chapter 4 I discussed my mother's illness and my spiritual transformation.

Near death experiences or NDEs are probably the best scientific proof of life after death; although skeptics think that they are nothing more than a game being played by the stressed brain. In Chapter 5 I discuss the fact that not all aspects of NDEs are scientifically understandable. In fact, most defy even the most logical neurobiological explanation. Therefore, in my opinion, NDEs indicate the actual existence of heaven or an afterlife.

In Chapter 6 I cover the research dealing with children who have past life memories, deathbed experiences, and after death communication, more evidence that the human soul is immortal. In Chapter 7 I attempt to address various scientific theories, such as the Big Bang and quantum mechanics, in order to show how and why they do not contradict the existence of God. Many great scientists, including Albert Einstein, have believed in God. In Chapter 7 I also delve into the numerous aspects of the Afterlife based on what I learned from my spiritual teachers.

Where appropriate I cite the original work of scientists who have been published in peer-reviewed scientific journals so that my readers can research these papers for themselves. I also list a number of excellent books that I highly recommend for further study.

I want to thank my wife Alice for putting up with me as I obsessed over this book, working long hours every evening and on the weekends. If my readers enjoy it my efforts will be rewarded.

Respectfully,
Amitava Dasgupta
Houston, Texas
November 2015

Brahma

Jehovah

1

WHY I AM A FALLEN HINDU

INTRODUCTION

Hinduism is the oldest religion in the world, with approximately one billion followers. Hinduism is also the third most popular world religion after Christianity and Islam. I was born to a religious Hindu mother and an atheist father in Calcutta (now Kolkata), India. Therefore it is not unexpected that I am neither an atheist nor a religious Hindu, but something in between, a "fallen" Hindu, or what I prefer to call a confused Hindu.

The earliest form of Hinduism originated in ancient India, most likely around 3000 BC, but the Vedas, the original scriptures of Hinduism, originated much later. The name "Hindu" derives from the Indus River, which currently flows through Pakistan and Northern India. The ancient name of this river was *Sindhu* in Sanskrit, but Persians pronounced Sindhu "Hindu." Thus the people who lived in the Indus valley became "Hindus."

"Hindu" is not a Sanskrit word and neither is "India." The latter comes from the Greeks: when Alexander invaded India the Macedonian army called the Sindhu River "Indos," and the land east of the Sindhu river "India."[1] It is believed that the people who lived in the ancient Indus valley were Aryans. Originally "Aryans" referred to people who spoke an Indo-European language, were fair skinned, and who settled in the Northern parts of India and Iran.

Archeological evidence indicates that there was an ancient society in the Indus valley known as the "Harappan" civilization, based on

---

1. Jayaraman V. "The Origin and Definition of the Name Hindu." www.hunduwebsite.com/hinduism/h_meaning.asp. Accessed June 12, 2015.

the name of the major city Harappa. Unfortunately the writings of this ancient people have not been deciphered, indicating that their chronicles were neither Sanskrit nor related to Sanskrit. The Harappans probably date back to 7000 BC, but the region did not become fully populated until around 2300-2000 BC. It has been speculated that Harappan society declined due to flooding, as well as invasion by Aryans—who suppressed the original language of the Harrapans.

The Vedas, the foundation of Hinduism, should be credited to those Aryans who immigrated to India. Aryans were probably a heterogeneous group of people who lived in different parts of the world, including Europe, the Mediterranean, Central Asia, and Northwestern parts of India. Aryans worshipped gods and goddesses in great religious fire ceremonies. They originally spoke a myriad of languages. Later these became part of the Indo-European language group, out of which Sanskrit itself probably originated.

Hinduism is far older than Christianity, with roots dating back to the Bronze Age (or earlier) some 5,000 years ago. Yet both share many common features.

Currently a number of scholars reject the Aryan-invasion-of-ancient-India theory, and consider "Aryan" little more than a social distinction. This is, in great part, because in Sanskrit Aryan means "noble" or "distinguished," while the word "Aryan Putra" means "son of a noble" or a "distinguished person." This word was frequently used in old Sanskrit epics and literature to refer to a prince or child of an aristocrat.

Hinduism differs from other major faiths, such as Christianity, Judaism, and Islam, in that it is more of a philosophy and a way of life rather than an actual religion. Furthermore, Hinduism has no founder, nor does it possess a single holy text like the Quran, the Torah, or the Bible, around which the faith coalesces. In fact, most forms of Hinduism are henotheistic; that is, they believe in a single Supreme Being, but also accept the existence of other deities as manifestations of the one Almighty God (in Sanskrit, *Brahman*). However, there is a school of philosophy in Hinduism that believes in only one God, showing that Hinduism has monotheistic elements that place it alongside Christianity and Islam.

Interestingly, in both Christianity and Islam God is the Supreme Being, so humans cannot be equal to God. But God loves us and after death he may forgive our sins, allowing our souls to live on in heaven, his own world. In contrast, in *Advaita* (a Sanskrit word meaning "non-dualism"), a philosophy of Hinduism, there is no distinction or duality between God and the human soul, except in our perception. Here, the entire universe is one reality called "God," and the rest is *maya* (Sanskrit, "illusion"). Therefore, it is our faulty perception that causes us to see God and ourselves as separate. According to other schools of Hindu philosophy, however, God (and other deities) and humans are indeed separate, because God, and even the lower gods and goddesses, are superior to humans. Therefore, humans must pray to appease these deities, and also work to create good karma throughout their lives in order to enter the kingdom of heaven.

Today most Hindus pray to one specific deity, or sometimes several of them. For example, my mother mostly prays to Lord Shiva, but also on certain auspicious days of the year she prays to Durga (the goddess of power and strength), Laxami (the goddess of wealth), and Saraswati (the goddess of learning and higher education). The Hindu religion is very complex and can be confusing, even to someone like me, who was born in a Hindu family and raised by a religious Hindu mother. Perhaps this is why I am fallen Hindu: my birth religion was too complicated for me.

For example, in modern Hinduism eating beef is considered a major sin because cows are sacred. However, ancient Hindus loved eating beef and during religious ceremonies bulls were sacrificed. Therefore, if in the Vedas eating beef is not condemned, why it is a sin today? Does God change his mind, or is it only Indian cows which are blessed? Is it okay to eat beef in the U.S. but not in India? Once I told our family priest that I do not eat beef in India. I only eat it in the U.S., because American cows are not blessed. As a Hindu, he was not pleased with my answer.

In this chapter I will explain why I adhere to the Hindu philosophy of living according to the principles of *Dharma* (a Sanskrit word meaning "religiously correct actions"), but do not believe in many of the Hindu superstitions, which I find meaningless. However, in order to explain why I am a fallen Hindu, I would first like to talk about the origin of religion, as well as the philosophical basis of the Hindu religion. In the process I will also touch on some of Hinduism's more ridiculous rituals, the reasons I do not respect these rituals, and why they helped lead to my falling away from the Hindu faith.

ORIGIN OF RELIGION

Archeologists consider the intentional human burials discovered during the period between 500,000 and 300,000 years ago to be the earliest evidence of religious ideas. In the most primitive cultures, the basic form of religion started with a belief that spiritual forces exist which pervade all creation.

The next step of development was "animism," a belief that spiritual forces underlie all events, and that objects of the physical world carry spiritual significance. In animism there are two types of spirits: ancestral spirits and nature spirits. It was held that nature spirits take human form and inhabit natural objects, such as plants, trees, rocks, hills, mountains, and lakes.

Throughout this period prehistoric people believed that there was a direct connection between the fertility of nature and the fertility of women, for the role of the male in human reproduction (paternity) was not yet known. The female's reproductive powers were thought to be parthenogenic, and therefore magical and all-powerful. Thus the first true religions were matriarchal, matrifocal, and matricentric in character, with the Supreme Being imaged as a woman. The archaeological record corroborates this: the earliest known artistic representations of "God" are female, usually shown (like the famed "Venus" figurines of Old Europe) with featureless faces, large pendulous breasts, swollen pudenda, and pregnant bellies. This female "God" was none other than the Great Mother-Goddess, venerated around the world under thousands of names. Artistic depictions of the Supreme Being as male are not found in the fossil record until much later.[2]

In the following stage of human evolution, dating from the Neolithic period (the "New Stone" Age, approximately 11,000 years ago), we find the beginnings of a more settled lifestyle, agriculture, and the development of more complex religious systems and beliefs. Neolithic religions were primarily polytheistic in nature (the belief in many gods and goddesses, along with the continuing growth of the worship of idols effigies, and images).

Writing was probably invented in ancient Mesopotamia around 3200 BC. In ancient times Egyptians practiced polytheism and believed in an afterlife. As a result they preserved dead bodies by mummification. In addition, large pyramids were constructed as tombs for the pharaohs who they thought became gods after death. Other ancient religions, such as those of the Greeks and Romans, were mostly polytheistic in nature.

Pantheism (the belief that all is God) has also prevailed as a major religious belief in many early civilizations. In pantheism individuals maintain that God is present everywhere and that everything in the cosmos, including the material world, is divine in nature. Therefore, it is important to live in harmony with nature. Spinoza was probably the first modern day philosopher to clearly introduce the concept of pantheism. He argued that everything that exists is God because God has infinite qualities, out of which we can perceive only a few. Later, Einstein was influenced by the philosophy of "Spinoza's God." Pantheism is still very much alive, even within Christianity.

Today most people embrace monotheism (only one God), a spiritual belief system that dates back to at least the time of the sun-worshipping ancient Egyptian pharaoh Akhenaten (1350 BC). Judaism, Christianity, and Islam trace their roots to a single ancestor, Abraham, and all three of these religions believe that human beings are the creation of a single God.

It is interesting to note that two major religions of the world, Christianity and Islam, originated in the Middle-East, while a third major

---

2. For more on the topics of matriarchy and thealogy (goddess-based religion), see Lochlainn Seabrook's books: *Britannia Rules: Goddess-worship in Ancient Anglo-Celtic Society*, Sea Raven Press, 2010; *The Book of Kelle: An Introduction to Goddess-worship and the Great Celtic Mother-Goddess Kelle*, Sea Raven Press, 2010; and *The Goddess Dictionary of Words and Phrases*, Sea Raven Press, 2010.

religion, Hinduism, arose in India. In addition, Judaism also originated in the Middle-East, while other popular religions, such as Buddhism and Jainism, were founded on the Indian sub-continent. These are the major religions practiced in the world today.

VARIOUS THEORIES EXPLAINING ORIGIN OF RELIGIONS

The German philosopher Max Muller (1823-1900) argued that religion originated out of myths and cults, which were based upon the personification of natural phenomena. According to Muller, the embodiment of nature (the sun, sky, mountains, stars, rocks, etc.) was the foundation of the earliest known spiritual beliefs. Philosopher Herbert Spencer (1820-1903) argued that religion originated out of the respect given to ancestors and, as a result, gods were derived from early savage experiences of ghosts, who were thought to be the heroic ancestors of a particular tribe or group.

Sir E. B. Taylor introduced the animistic theory of religion. Animism (from the Latin word *animus*, meaning "spirit") was a belief that nonhuman entities (animals, plants, and inanimate objects) also have souls. Animism was the fundamental supernatural belief system of prehistoric tribes long before the emergence of organized religion. Animism and ancestor worship eventually transformed into polytheism and eventually monotheism.

French sociologist Emile Durkheim (1858-1917) argued that religion originated in totemic rites that were designed to promote the social solidarity of a given tribe. In totemism each individual is believed to have a spiritual connection or a kinship with another physical being, such as an animal or plant, often called a "spirit-being" or "totem." Thus a totem is a spirit being, sacred object, or symbol of a tribe, clan, family or individual. It can also be a species of animal, plant, or more rarely a class of inanimate objects to which clan members have a special relationship. A totem is not exactly God, but something which is highly respected by the tribe. To this day many native peoples continue to practice totemism.

Sigmund Freud (1856-1939), the father of psychoanalysis, provided the theory of the psychological origin of religion in his writings; *Totem and Taboo* (1913), *The Future of An Illusion* (1928), *Civilization and its Discontents* (1930) and *Moses and Monotheism* (1939). In his opinion religion is an expression of the underlying psychological neurosis, fears, and wretchedness of mankind.[3]

In social psychology, "Terror Management Theory" (TMT) deals with a basic human conflict: we want to live forever, but mortality is unavoidable. Animals live in the present and cannot comprehend mortality, but highly evolved humans know that one day death is inevitable. The concept of TMT may be derived from anthropologist Ernest Baker's Pulitzer Prize winning book *The Denial of Death*, where the author argued that all humans are instinctively driven towards survival, while at the same time having knowledge of their inescapable mortality.[4] As a result, only humans are terrified by the thought of death, and cope with this fear by taking refuge in religious beliefs which hold that the human soul lives on for eternity after earthly "death."

All religions assure an afterlife and eternal existence of the soul. In addition, Hinduism, Buddhism, and Jainism believe in reincarnation, an assurance that each individual will transcend death. Krause and Hayward reported lower death anxiety among individuals who felt forgiven by God.[5] However, atheist Karl Marx (1818-1883) famously declared that "religion is the opiate of the masses," and explained religion as an epiphenomenon arising from an economic foundation and a control mechanism to harness the labor force. I encapsulate the various theories on the origins of religion in Table 1 at the end of this chapter.

GOD AND THE HUMAN BRAIN

The human brain is a wonder of human evolution, consisting of 100 billion neurons (nerve cells) with an estimated storage capacity of 1.25×10^{12} bytes, indicating that cognitive capacity of the human brain is virtually limitless. The latest stage of the human brain was the development of the neocortex. When humans learn new things, the chemistry of neurons in the neocortex area is altered.[6]

Approximately 2 million years ago the brain size of prehistoric people was 400-600 cubic centimeters (cc). During early human

---

3. Wallace ER 4th. "Freud and Religion." Am J Psychiatry 1979; 136: 237-238.
4. Earnest Baker. *Denial of Death*. Free Press, 1997.
5. Krause N, Hayward RD. "Religious Involvement and Death Anxiety." Omega (Westpoint) 2014; 69: 59-78.
6. Hofman MA. "Evolution of the Human Brain: When Bigger is Better." Front Neuroanat 2014; 8:15.

evolution, approximately 500,000 years ago, much of the brain's expansion took place in the neocortex region and began approaching the size of a modern human being. At that time the neocortex was large enough to process complex social phenomena, such as symbolic language and religion. Therefore, the concept of religion in ancient man was related to the evolutionary development of the neocortex.

Various regions of the brain have been implicated in religious experiences. Morality is the most sophisticated feature of human judgement and behavior. Young et al reported that the ventromedial prefrontal cortex is critical for human morality.[7] Morality and religious beliefs are sometimes interconnected. Wain and Spinella noted that the prefrontal cortex plays an important role in morality, religion, and paranormal beliefs. Hyper-religiosity may be related to hyper-function of the medial prefrontal cortex.[8]

The limbic system, which is located at the top of the brainstem, and consists of the amygdala, thalamus, hypothalamus, and hippocampus, is considered the emotional center of the brain. This system plays an important role in the perception of God and religion. The amygdala and inferior temporal lobe appear to be developed in Neanderthal, Cro-Magnon, and other early humans, enabling them to have religious and spiritual beliefs. The activation of neurons in the amygdala-temporal lobe is associated with religious feelings. It has been postulated that the neurons responsible for religious/mystical experiences evolved by 30,000 years ago, or maybe even 100,00 years

Jesus teaching the secrets of not the "Gospel of Christ," but the "Gospel of the Kingdom of God" to his disciples in the Galilean countryside.

---

7. Young L, Koenigs M. "Investigating Emotion in Moral Recognition: A Review of Evidence From Functional Neuroimaging and Neuropsychology." Br. Med Bull 2007; 84: 69-79.
8. Wain O, Spinella M. "Executive Functions in Morality, Religion and Paranormal Beliefs." Int J Neurosci 2007; 117: 135-148.

ago[9] (though evidence of forms of primitive spiritual thought has been found dating back to at least 500,000 years ago).[10]

Several investigators consider the temporal lobe as another center of the brain, one that is responsible for religious experiences. Schjoedt et al, using the magnetic resonance imaging technique (MRI), observed that praying activates a strong response in the temporal region, the medial prefrontal cortex, the tempo-parietal junction, and the precuneus (a structure in the parietal lobe of the brain near the juncture between the two hemispheres). Therefore, for a religious person, praying to God or being connected to God is an interpersonal interaction, similar to the normal interpersonal interaction between two people in a social context.[11]

In their book *God's Brain*, Lionel Tiger, the Charles Darwin Professor of Anthropology at Rutgers University, and distinguished neuroscientist Michael McGuire, hypothesized that humans are affected by unavoidable sources of stress in daily life, which the authors describe as "brain pain." To cope with this discomfort humans seek the secretion of serotonin, a neurotransmitter, to sooth the brain. Therefore, religious belief may be an evolutionary drive in which humans strive to achieve emotional well-being. Attending a religious service can induce the release of several neurotransmitters, including serotonin.[12] Serotonin deficiency in the brain may cause depression, and antidepressants, such as SSRI (Selective Serotonin Reuptake Inhibitors, for example, Prozac), restores the serotonin level in the brain in order to alleviate depression.

Serotonin may have played a crucial role in the enlightenment experience of Siddhartha Goutam (Buddha), who was the founder of the Buddhist religion 2500 years ago. He practiced meditation for a long time and his body reached a state of extreme starvation. Then a passerby, a woman named Sujata, offered him rice pudding. After eating it Siddhartha started meditating again and effortlessly experienced enlightenment. Paul Joseph published an interesting hypothesis

---

9. Joseph R. "The Limbic System and the Soul." *Zygon: The Journal of Religion and Science*, 2001; 36: 105-136.
10. Lochlainn Seabrook. *The Goddess Dictionary of Words and Phrases*. Sea Raven Press, 2010, p. 18.
11. Schjoedt U, Stodkilde-Jorgensen H, Geertz AW, Roepstorff A. "Highly Religious Participants Recruit Area of Social Cognition in Personal Prayer." Soc Cogn Affect Neurosci 2009; 4: 199-207.
12. Lionel Tiger, Michael McGuire. *God's Brain*. Prometheus Books, 2010.

explaining the enlightenment experience of Siddhartha as a known medical phenomenon referred to as "refeeding syndrome." Here the specific content of the food he ate (rice pudding, containing high tryptophan and high carbohydrate but low protein) played a key role in his enlightenment experience.

For Siddhartha, intense fasting inhibited his MAO (monoamine oxidase, an enzyme which degrades serotonin) activity, but eating rice pudding constituted an intake of dietary tryptophan and carbohydrates from milk and rice, which increased tryptophan in his brain, which was eventually converted into serotonin. Because Siddhartha's MAO activity was inhibited due to prolonged starvation, the serotonin generated in his brain following eating rice pudding did not degrade. As a result he experienced enlightenment.[13]

In addition to serotonin another neurotransmitter, dopamine, also plays a role in religious experience. Previc commented that the evolution of religion is linked to an expansion of the dopaminergic system during human evolution.[14]

In Dean Hamer's book, *The God Gene: How Faith is Hardwired in Our Genes*, the author proposes that the religiosity of an individual is influenced by one's genetic makeup. He also proposed that the VMAT2 gene is one of many potential genes that impinge spirituality in a person. In addition, one particular variation (polymorphism) in the gene is associated with more spirituality.[15]

Dreams are a source of spiritual ideas. For example, the concept of a supernatural agent may have originated from the dreams of prehistoric people. Some individuals claim that during sleep the dreamer's soul wanders outside the body and communicates with spirits and or God. In some traditional Polynesian cultures it is believed that during dreaming we connect with sacred ancestors.

Significant anthropological evidence links the belief in supernatural agents with dreams. It has been postulated that human beings first conceived of the idea of a spirit realm because they

---

13. Joseph PG. "Serotonergic and Tryptaminergic Overstimulation on Refeeding Implicated 'Enlightenment' Experience." Med Hypotheses 2012; 79: 598-601.
14. Previc FH. "The Role of the Extrapersonal Brain System in Religious Activity." *Consciousness Cognition* 2006; 15: 500-539.
15. Dean H. Hamer. *The God Gene: How Faith is Hardwired into Our Genes*. Anchor Books, 2005.

experienced it during sleep. During sleep rapid eye movement (REM) and non-rapid eye movement (NREM) our sleep state alternates throughout the night. Dreams may be different during REM and NREM sleep, and the recognition of supernatural agents also differ in relation to the sleep state. However, religious dreams probably take place during REM sleep.[16]

HINDU RELIGIOUS SCRIPTURES

In order to help explain why I am a fallen Hindu, I will now provide an overview of Hindu religious texts and the practice of modern Hinduism.

In contrast to Christianity (founded by Jesus Christ) and Islam (founded by the Prophet Muhammad), Hinduism has no founder. The four Vedas (in Sanskrit Veda means "knowledge") are considered the most ancient scriptures of Hinduism. Another name for the Vedas is *sutri* (a Sanskrit word meaning "what is heard"). Orthodox Hindus believe that the Vedas were not written by humans, and that the Vedic mantras (hymns) were divinely revealed to Indian saints (Sanskrit, *rishis*). Therefore, the Vedas are seen as *apaurashaya* (Sanskrit, "not created by humans"). The Vedas, which were transmitted orally from teacher to disciples, consisted of hymns, charms, spells, and ritual observations. But over time many of these teachings were lost and the versions we have today certainly differ significantly from the originals. The original Vedas, which probably originated between 1700 and 800 BC, are four in number: the Rig-Veda, the Sama-Veda, the Yajur-Veda, and the Atharva-Veda.

The Rig-Veda originated approximately between 1700-1100 BC (Bronze Age). Verses from it are still recited in Hindu religious ceremonies. The Rig-Veda is full of mythological and poetic accounts of the origin of the world, hymns praising various gods and goddess, as well as prayers for prosperity, wealth, and happiness. The Rig-Vedic hymns were dedicated to various gods, including *Indra*, the king of heaven, *Vishnu*, *Rudra*, *Brishaspati*, *Agni* (sacrificial fire), *Surya* (the sun god), etc. Certain natural phenomenon, such as dawn (Sanskrit, *Usha*), wind

---

16. McNamara P, Bulkeley K. "Dreams as a Source of Supernatural Agent Concept." Frontiers Psychology 2015; 6: 1-8.

(Sanskrit, *Vayu*), and thunder (Sanskrit, *Parjanya*) were also worshipped.

The modern version of the Rig-Veda contains 1017 hymns, though some have been lost. Most melodies in the Sama-Veda were borrowed from the Rig-Veda. The Yajur-Veda served as a guidebook for priests who performed Hindu religious ceremonies, including sacrifices during the Vedic period. Some scholars believe that the Yajur-Vedas originated after the Rig-Veda, but before the Sama-Veda. The Atharva-Veda is different from the other Vedas because it contains accounts of magic and healing traditions that are similar to those found in other types of Indo-European literature. It was also the last of all the Vedas to have originated in ancient India.

The religious practices in the Vedic age rested on a priest who performed various rites often involving sacrifices. *Homa* (a Sanskrit word meaning "ceremonial fire") was an integral part of *Yagna* (a Sanskrit word for Hindu religious ritual), where offerings were made to God. Although a consecrated fire was the central element of every *homa* ritual, the procedure and items offered to the fire varied depending on which particular Vedic god was being worshipped. Procedures invariably involved animal sacrifices. One of the most highly acclaimed rituals was *Ashwamedha Yagna*, which only a powerful king was allowed to perform. *Ashwa* in Sanskrit means "horse" and *medha* in Sanskrit means "killing."

During *Ashwamedha Yagna*, a special horse was allowed to roam freely in neighboring kingdoms, accompanied by the army of the emperor who was to perform the ritual. The rulers of those countries in which the horse wandered had to accept the supremacy of the emperor who sent it. After one year, when the horse returned to the kingdom of the emperor, a grand religious ceremony was performed in which it was sacrificed. It is said that as part of the ritual the chief queen engaged in sexual congress with the dead animal (while some scholars take this literally, others hold that it was merely a simulation with a live horse, after which it was set free). Many other animals were also sacrificed during *Ashwamedha Yagna*, and the public was allowed to attend and witness these rituals.

There was once a nude worship ritual in the Southern part of India. The *bettale seve* (nude worship) was a form of veneration rendered while naked to the goddess Renukamba at Chandragutti, Shimoga, in central Karnatake. Most women who participated in it were from the

Dalit-Bahujan caste (lower caste). This rite was meant to honor the goddess who fulfilled a wish of the devotee (such as bearing a child or getting married, etc.). As part of the ritual the worshipper would bathe in the River Varada and walk five kilometers (approximately 3 miles) naked, finally entering the temple for prayer. The bettale seve was performed only once a year, during the month of March. Fortunately, the practice was banned on March 4, 2003.[17]

The late Vedic period marked the beginning of the Upanisadic or Vedantic period. The Upanishads are a continuation of the Vedic philosophy, and were composed between 800 and 400 BC. There are more than 200 Upanishads, but the Brhadaranyaka and the Chandogya are the two earliest, and were probably composed between the 7th and 6th Centuries BC, just before the birth of Buddha. The three other early Upanishads, the Taittiriya, the Aitareya, and the Kausitaki, were probably also pre-Buddhist in origin, and were composed between the 6th and 5th Centuries BC.

During this period Hindus began deviating from the elaborate rituals of Yagans, and focusing more on the practice of meditation and other simple rites in order to connect with God. The Upanishads elaborated practical ways on how the soul (Sanskrit, *Atman*) can unite with the supreme God (Brahman) through mediation and good deeds (Sanskrit, *karma*). In the later part of this period the Sanskrit epics (the Ramayana and the Mahabharata), and the Puranas (a Sanskrit word meaning "ancient") were composed. However, the Upanishads represent the core of Hindu philosophy.

The Ramayana (the "Story of Rama") was written by the sage Valmiki, probably between 400 and 200 BC. The Ramayana contained seven chapters, with a total of 24,000 verses. The Mahabharata, meaning "Great India," was written by Vyasa, between 400 and 100 BC, an epic containing 18 chapters and over 100,000 verses. A story incorporated into the Mahabharata became known as the Bhagavad Gita, which many Hindus call simply "Gita." The Puranas typically described the creation of the universe and its possible destruction, and included numerous stories about various kings, heroes, and demigods. Well

---

17. *The Hindu Newspaper*, March 4th, 2003. Title of article, "Nude worship banned."

known Puranas are the Brahma Puran, the Vishnu Puran and the Shiva Puran.

One of the founding religious texts of Hinduism is the Bhagavad Gita, meaning "Songs of the God." The Bhagavad Gita consists of 18 chapters and 700 verses written in the form of a conversation between Krishna and Arjuna on the battlefield of Kurukshetra (an epic conflict described in the Mahabharata) prior to the start of the holy war (Sanskrit, *Dharma Yudha*). Arjuna was reluctant to participate because he did not want to kill his opponents, who happened to be his cousins, merely to recover the kingdom. At this point, Krishna, the charioteer, explains to Arjuna his duties as a warrior, and educates him on the Vedantic philosophies, while revealing his true identity as an incarnation of Lord Vishnu. After realizing Krishna's true form, Arjuna agreed to fight, and finally his side (Pandavas) won the battle.

The author, Amitava Dasgupta, in front of the Taj Mahal, at Agra, Uttar Pradesh, India, in 1999.

A major teaching of the Gita is that the soul is immortal and that every human being should engage in good karma (daily actions of life) without any expectation of a favorable result (Sanskrit phrase, *nishkam karma*, meaning "selfless action"). An example of *nishkam karma* is to work very hard at a job without expecting any salary increase or even a tiny bit of praise from your boss. In the Bhagavad Gita Krishna explains three different approaches to breaking the cycle of life and death, with the ultimate goal of God realization. These three practices include giving complete devotion to God (Sanskrit, *bhakti-yoga*), selfless and desire-less action (*nishkam karma* or *karma-yoga*), and walking the path of knowledge in order to comprehend the true nature of God (Sanskrit, *Jnana-yoga*). Krishna did not disregard the physical world, but advised everyone to live in harmony with the divine laws.

HOW A HINDU SHOULD LIVE

In the ancient Vedic period (1700 BC-500 BC) religious rituals (*Yagna*) were an integral part of the practice of Hinduism. But due to the enormous cost, only kings and very wealthy people were able to conduct such rituals. Then, in the post Vedic period (500-200 BC) Buddhism and Jainism evolved in India as major religions, offering alternative pathways for spiritual growth. The more expensive *Yagnas* lost their glory and the common people became more focused on individual worship or group worship.

In sharp contrast to *Yagnas*, where many animals were sacrificed, both Buddhism and Jainism preached nonviolence to all living creatures, and killing animals, even for food, was rigorously prohibited in both religions. To this day the followers of Jainism in India are strict vegetarians, as are many Buddhists. Although ancient Hindus ate meat, many Hindus today are also vegetarians. Some scholars think that this is due to the influence of Jainism.

Some of the concepts of the Hindu religion, for example, reincarnation, were not mentioned in the Rig-Veda or other ancient texts, but became a part of the Hindu belief system later. Interestingly, both Buddhism and Jainism endorse the concept of reincarnation. Buddha, during his enlightenment, observed his previous incarnations, which were depicted in approximately 550 stories in a sacred Buddhist text known as the "Tales of Jataka." These texts were probably written between 300 BC and AD 400, after his death. Interestingly, in some tales Buddha incarnated as a animal, in others as a human. Many of these stories were set in or near Varanasi, an ancient holy city in India located on the bank of the River Ganges.

There are four goals (all Sanskrit words) for a Hindu person; *Dharma* (religiously correct action), *Artha* (wealth), *Kama* (desire or sexual pleasure), and *Moksha* (God realization and breaking the cycle of birth and death). Dharma is right action based on the moral codes of religious teachings. According to the principles of Dharma, a person should live for the benefit of others, and always perform selfless acts (*nishkam karma*). Money and wealth (*artha*) are important for living, but money should be earned in an honest way, following moral and ethical codes. Moreover, money should be wisely spent to benefit others, not merely to fulfill one's own desires.

According to the teachings of the modern day Indian saint Ramakrishna, making lots of money or being wealthy is perfectly fine. But only as long as one considers this money a gift from God, one to be used not only to take care of his/her family and friends, but also strangers who are less fortunate. When a wealthy person becomes arrogant and denies God, then he or she is following the wrong path.

Kama literally means "sexual pleasure," which for most is an integral part of life. Hindus are encouraged to marry and raise children, but the practice of monogamy is essential. *Moksha* means "liberation" or "breaking the cycle of life and death." A person who lives following moral codes and performs selfless acts (*nishkam karma*) will be rewarded by Moksha.

Hindu people typically come to a temple (*mandir*) for worship, and different temples have different deities. Moreover, each house may also have a shrine in a room which contains one deity or more. A priest may come every day for worship (*puja*) or on auspicious days, but an individual can also pray or perform puja. During puja, fruits, vegetables, and or sweets are offered to the deity, and after the ceremony every one present will eat the blessed offerings (*prasad*). Sometimes a person may simply pray, which is also a form of puja, without any offering to a deity or deities. Sometimes specials pujas are performed during religious festivals.

CASTE SYSTEM IN HINDUISM

The caste system is a typical feature of the Hindu religion, dividing society into four categories; *Brahmins* (highest class, only Brahmins can act as a priest for religious ceremonies), *Kshatriyas* (warrior class), *Vaishyas* (merchants), and *Shudras* (working class). It was said in the Puranas (an ancient text, but written after the Vedas) that Lord Brahma (the ultimate creator of the universe) created some humans from his mouth and they became Brahmins because they were reciters of the Vedas. Afterward Brahma created other humans from his arms

(Kshatriyas, the warrior and ruling class). Lord Brahma created Vaishyas (merchants or people involved in trade) from his abdomen and finally created Shudras (manual labors) from his feet. However, the stories found in the Puranas are considered mythological.

In ancient India, the caste system (6th to 3rd Century BC) was not rigid: a man born to a lower caste could be elevated to the Brahmin class by showing the high moral standard and knowledge expected of a Brahmin. Valmiki, the writer of the epic Ramayana, was born as a Shudra, but by virtue of the long tedious practice of meditation, he was elevated to the highest caste.

The Hindu epic Mahabharata declares that one's birth ancestry should not decide whether one is a Brahmin or not. Other ancient Hindu texts cite numerous examples of individuals moving from the lower caste to the Brahmin caste within their lifetimes.

The story of Satyakama-Jabala, for instance, appears in the Chandogya Upanishad. Satyakama wanted to study under Rishi Gautama (not Gautama Siddhartha), and asked his mother about his father. Unfortunately, his mother Jabala was a prostitute, and did not know who the father was. When Satyakama went to see Rishi Gautama, he fearlessly acknowledged that he was born as an illegitimate child. Rishi Gautama was impressed by Satyakama's honesty, and announced that only a Brahmin could be so truthful. He accepted Satyakama as his student.

Later, in the 18th Century, however, especially during British rule, the caste system became a serious problem in Hinduism. At this time people of the higher caste began regarding people of the lower caste as subhuman, and the term "untouchable" entered the vocabulary. Saint Ramakrishna rebelled against the Indian caste system, announcing that everyone is the same in the eyes of God. He also declared that God realization can be achieved by following any religion, because all religious paths are valid and any one of them can reveal the ultimate truth. Swami Vivekananda, a Hindu monk and the chief disciple of the 19th-Century saint Ramakrishna, introduced the Indian philosophies of Vedanta and Yoga to the Western world in his famous speech at the Parliament of the World's Religions in Chicago in 1893. He later founded the Ramakrishna Mission, which is a major spiritual center for the study of Hinduism in India, with many branches throughout the world. The Ramakrishna Mission is also known for its charity work, as well as having an educational mission with many high quality schools and colleges in India, where the criteria of admission is based strictly on merit.

Swami Vivekananda did not believe in untouchability, and started a movement in India to the end caste system. Later Mahatma Gandhi, who was born into a wealthy merchant family and completed his legal education in London, also sought to abolish the concept of human untouchability—although he is best known for achieving India's freedom through his nonviolent movement.

After independence from Britain, Indian law banned discrimination against the lower castes, although in rural areas prejudice and sometimes violence, against the lower castes is still reported. In metropolitan cities and urban areas this type of discrimination is less common. During modern arranged marriages the caste system can still play a role; but when marriages are not arranged and people fall in love, parents of both the groom and the bride usually accept inter-caste unions—although there are exceptions.

CASTE SYSTEM AND GENETIC STUDY

Based on genetic studies it has been postulated that the caste system in India was probably firmly established by about 2,000 years ago. Genetic evidence indicates that the current Indian population descends from a mixture of two divergent ancestral populations: *ancestral North Indian*, related to West Eurasians (people from Central Asia, the Middle East, and Europe) and *ancestral South Indian*, related distantly to the people of the Andaman Islands.

The Hindi language, which is spoken in North India, is derived from Sanskrit, an Indo-European language, while Tamil and Telugu, spoken widely in South India, derive from Dravidian languages. Today everyone in India has DNA from both groups due to the initial mixing of the population, but the amount of DNA inherited from individual groups varies across India.

Moorjani et al analyzed DNA from 371 people who were members of 73 groups throughout the Indian subcontinent, and postulated that approximately 4,200 years ago or earlier, two groups in India probably lived side by side without intermarriage. However, by around 1900-4200 years ago, a period of demographic and cultural change took place in India, characterized by the de-urbanization of the Indus Valley civilization, population mixing due to intermarriage, shifting of the population along the Ganges River, and migration in Southern India.

Early on there were three distinct classes of people in India: the priests, the noble people, and the common people. Although the four castes (Sanskrit, *varna*) comprised of Brahmin, Kshatriyas, Vaisyas, and Shudra, were mentioned in the Vedas, the concept of the Shudra emerged approximately 3000 years ago. Moreover, there was no mention of the social and occupational roles of the various castes in the Rig-Veda. The authors speculate that inter-caste marriages stopped approximately 2000 years ago when the caste system was firmly endorsed in India. This was most likely due to a holy text called the Manu Samhita (written 100 BC), which explicitly forbade intermarriage across castes. As a result, caste divisions hardened and any type of intermarriage was sharply curtailed, leading to much less mixing between populations, as evidenced by genetic analysis.[18]

DIALECTICAL MATERIALISM IN HINDUISM

Dialectical materialism is the philosophical expression of Karl Marx, Frederick Engels, and Marxism-Leninism. This philosophy is a materialistic view of the world that denies the existence of God. Interestingly long before Marx and Engels, a Hindu philosopher named Rishi Charvak introduced a material worldview.

Charvak's philosophy disclaimed the existence of God and compared the sacred religious texts of the Vedas to "one blind man leading another." As a result, Charvak was persecuted by religious leaders and very little written by him was preserved. It has been conjectured that he was a major threat to Hinduism, and as a result his writings were destroyed by religious authorities with the support of the king. However, what has been recovered show that his major philosophical beliefs included the following:

---

18. Moorjani P, Thangaraj K, Patterson N, Loh PR et al. "Genetic Evidence for Recent Population Mixture in India." Am J Hum Genet 2013; 93: 422-438.

- God does not exist.
- The concept of heaven and hell is an illusion.
- The concept of reincarnation is false.
- It is a waste of time and money to participate in religious ceremonies. A person should focus on the material aspects of life, such as farming, animal husbandry, or business.
- The aim of human existence is not to achieve the illusionary *moksha*, but to look for happiness in life.

Although an atheist, Charvak had high moral principles and declared that public service is an important aspect of living in harmony with society. He also taught that death is ultimately an annihilation, because when the body is cremated and turned into ashes, one has crossed the point of no return. Here is one of his more famous sayings:

Jabat jivet sukham jivet runam krutya ghrutam pibeyat

Translation: "As long as you live, live happily and if necessary borrow money to include ghee (a special kind of butter) in your meal."

WHY I HAVE FALLEN AWAY FROM HINDUISM

The Hinduism that is practiced today is full of superstitions that did not come from its original holy texts. Thus, I do not follow many of the rituals of Hinduism, and my aunt, who is a devout Hindu, considers me a "fallen Hindu." I accept this evaluation.

I will now list a number of Hindu teachings and superstitions that I do not accept, embrace, or practice.

A. I do not believe in the existence of the 330 million gods and goddess of the Hindu religion. I believe in only one God.
Comments: Indra is the greatest god of the Rig-Veda. There are about 250 hymns addressed to Indra in the Rig-Veda, which represents one-fourth of all hymns. The Vedas mention 33 gods and goddesses that include eight Vasus, eleven Rudras, twelve Adityas, Dyaus, and Prithvi. The question is, how did modern Hinduism managed to accrue 330 million gods and goddess, which is more than the entire population of many countries in the world?

One explanation is that in the Vedas the word *koti* was mentioned after the names of the deities, which probably meant something else, but in modern Sanskrit *koti* means "10 million." Therefore, the 33 original gods and goddess became 330 million gods and goddesses.

The Christian Cross is merely a variation of a prehistoric symbol signifying the sacred number four, which in turn represents the four seasons, the four compass points, the four stages of life, the four elements, etc. In early Christian art it gave rise to the Tetramorph, which featured the Four Evangelists as the four fixed sun-signs in astrology: Matthew as Aquarius, Mark as Leo, Luke as Taurus, and John as Aquila (later Scorpio), iconography that can still be seen in many medieval Christian structures, such as Chartres Cathedral in France.

Moreover, many Hindu gods and goddesses came in from mythological texts, like the Puranas, and also due to the mixing of Aryans with the indigent people of India (often called non-Aryan). Many of the gods and goddesses of modern Hinduism have tribal origins, for example, the "dark" goddess Kali—whose fame spread all the way to Ireland (where she gave her name to the Irish goddess Kelle as well as to the Kelts/Celts themselves) and the Americas (where she gave her name to the state of California).[19]

B. I do not believe that only Hindus go to heaven.

Comments: I maintain that any person, regardless of religion, and even atheists, can and will go to heaven. However, I believe in the laws of karma and try to engage in good karma. Although ancient Vedic texts do not claim the supremacy of Hinduism over any other philosophy, some fundamentalist Hindus today believe that only Hinduism explains the mystery of the universe, and that only faithful Hindus have a passport to heaven. The fundamentalists of other religions share a similar belief. I believe any good person who lives a positive selfless life can go to heaven, and that

---

19. Lochlainn Seabrook. *The Book of Kelle: An Introduction to Goddess-worship and the Great Celtic Mother-Goddess Kelle*. Sea Raven Press, 2010, p. 70, passim.

includes nonbelievers.

C. I do not believe in the caste system.
Comments: Although the caste system was not strictly enforced before 100 BC, I think in the Vedic period it was strictly based on a division of labor. I do not believe that Brahmins are superior to Shudras, because as Saint Peter said, "God is no respecter of persons" (that is, all humans are the same in God's eyes).[20] A human being should be judged only by his qualities and character, not by his/her family's name, skin color, or nationality.

D. I do not consider the cow to be a holy animal.
Comments: In ancient India, oxen and bulls were sacrificed to the gods and their meat was eaten, though the slaughter of milk-producing cows was prohibited. Verses in the Rig Veda refer to the cow as Devi (goddess), identified with Aditi (the mother of the gods and goddesses).

However, even when meat-eating was permitted, the ancient Vedic scriptures encouraged vegetarianism. Therefore, it could be assumed that due to the influence of Buddhism and Jainism (both religions preach nonviolence), Hindus stopped eating oxen and bulls.

Some scholars indeed believe that the tradition of vegetarianism came to Hinduism through the influence of the strictly vegetarian aspect of Jainism. Many Hindus are vegetarian. In addition, the vegetarian diet is gaining popularity throughout the world. I respect vegetarians who do not believe in slaughtering animals for food, but I do not believe cows are sacred animals.

E. I do not believe that praying to a Hindu deity is a ticket to heaven.
Comments: I believe that the law of karma prevails and that living a good life, following ethical and moral standards, is of the utmost importance. If I feel like it, I go to a Hindu temple once in a while. But I do not believe that regularly praying to a deity is enough to secure a ticket to heaven. God is not an insurance policy. I am judged by my work.

If I repent for wrongdoing, I may be forgiven, but at the same

---

20. Acts 10:34.

time I believe that petitioning God through prayer, then deliberately engaging in bad karma, is wrong and is always punished. A faithful person should pray every day to connect with God. But not to bribe God so that he/she can deliberately do evil. We all make mistakes, and mistakes can only be forgiven when we sincerely repent.

F. I do not believe that as a Hindu I must marry a Hindu.
Comments: I do not believe that I am obligated to marry someone from the same religion. Marriage is a sacred union between a man and woman, and God is love. Therefore, I should marry a woman I love. My wife is a Christian and we have been happily married for 16 years. I have never tried to convert her to Hinduism and she has never attempted to convert me to Christianity. She believes Jesus is her savior, attends Church almost every Sunday, and donates money to charity. I believe she will go straight to heaven due to her goodness.

G. I do not believe bathing in the River Ganges can free me from sin.
Comments: Many Hindus believe that the Ganges has the power to wash away sins when one bathes in it. Moreover, on certain auspicious days, bathing in the river can guarantee one entrance into heaven. *Kumbh Mela* is a mass Hindu pilgrimage of faith in which Hindus gather to bathe in a sacred river (the Ganges and other sacred rivers). Approximately 80 million people attend this event. By rotation, it is held every third year at one of the four places: Haridwar (the River Ganges), Allahabad (Prayaga; the confluence of the Ganges, the Yamuna, and the mythical Saraswati River), Nashik (the Godavari River), and Ujjain (the Shipra River).

Kumbha means "pitcher" in Sanskrit. According to the myth, after *samudra monthan* (the churning of the ocean) by both gods and demons, *amrita* (the nectar of immortality) emerged, but the gods did not want to share it with the demons. When Indra's son was fleeing with the pitcher containing amrita, a few drops leaked out and fell on four places on earth (Haridwar, Allahabad, Nashik and Ujjain), which imbued these places with mystical powers.

The pilgrimage is held for about one and a half months at each of these four places. Here the people immerse themselves in the rivers with the hope that they will be cleansed of all sin. However, I believe I am responsible for my actions, and that the water of the River Ganges does not have the power to wash away my sins.

H. I do not believe that a Hindu widow should only wear a white sari and eat vegetarian meals.
Comments: Women had high status in the Vedic period, and in some ancient texts (the Tantric texts) it was stated that the male's power is worthless until the feminine power (Sanskrit, *Shakti*) activates it. In the Vedic period female goddesses, such as Durga, were worshipped as the symbol of ultimate power. However, starting about 100 BC the elevated status of women in Hindu society started to decline, and by the medieval period women were much lower on the social ladder than men.

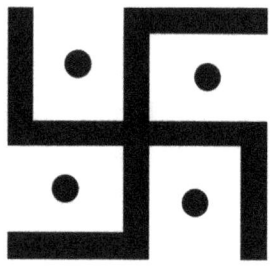

Thousands of years before the four-armed Christian Cross appeared, prehistoric people were drawing it on cave walls in the form of a swirling four-armed wheel of fire. This solar symbol was later absorbed into Hinduism as the *svastika*, a Sanskrit word meaning "so be it." This gives the swastika the same meaning as the English Christian word "amen," which itself is a variation of the Egyptian word "Amon" and the Hindu "Om." Hitler's adoption and distortion of the swastika does not change its original meaning as a Hindu symbol of love, good luck, health, regeneration, and eternal life.

One of the worst customs in Hinduism was *Sati* (Suttee in English), where a living widow was forced to be burned on the funeral pyre of her dead husband. Although this suicidal custom was purely voluntary, in most cases widows were forced by being tightly bound to the pyre so that they could not escape after it was lit. Moreover, society tried to convince the widow that this act would guarantee a spot for her in heaven forever, along with her husband. The real reason, however, was to deny the widow her rightful ownership of her deceased husband's property.

Only glorified examples of Sati tradition are found in the history of Rajasthan. Jauhar (also spelled jowhar) is referred to in rituals during the medieval period: to avoid being raped by invaders, queens and the female royals of Rajput kingdoms committed suicide by jumping into a sacred fire when facing defeat at the hands of enemy.

Although several Mughal emperors in India attempted to stop the brutal custom of Sati, Raja Ram Mohan Roy (1772-1833), a Hindu scholar and social reformer, finally convinced the British Government to legally ban the custom. As a result, a new Sati law was passed in 1829, making the burning of widows a criminal offense. Despite the ban, the Sati ritual has continued, though at lower rates, and mostly in remote areas of India. In 1987 a Rajput man was arrested after the sati death of his daughter-in-law, Roop Kanwar, who was only 18 years old and had only been married to her husband, Maal Singh, for eight months. The most tragic aspect of the story was that no one was punished, because on January 31, 2004, a special court in Jaipur acquitted all 11 defendants charged with the crime.[21]

Although the tradition of Sati has been abolished by law (Indian law also forbids it), Hindu widows are not allowed to eat non-vegetarian meals, and they must fast on some auspicious days at least twice a month. Moreover, they must wear a white sari, avoid the use of makeup, and are disbarred from wedding ceremonies. One of the reasons for this kind of torture is to make widows malnourished, which reduces their life spans, for widows are unwanted by their families. These traditions are cruel and purely superstitious, yet even today some Hindu widows still practice them.

After the death of my father on July 31, 2011, my mother insisted on following a strict vegetarian diet, despite my objection. However, changing her diet from non-vegetarian to vegetarian at the age of 82 took a heavy toll on her health, and she developed an ulcer. Following the recommendation of our physician, I forced her to eat fish, and also convinced her that committing suicide is against not only the Hindu religion, but all religions. Mother has a Master's degree and she worked for 35 years as a high school teacher. Despite her education, for a brief time she followed this illogical tradition. Moreover, she only eats fish now, but before being a widow she ate chicken and goat meat. This indicates how deep-rooted many superstitions are in Hinduism.

I. A Hindu should only travel long distances, start a new business, buy property, marry, etc., on auspicious days.
Comments: Auspicious dates and times for various activities are

---

21. John Stratton Hawley (ed.). *Sati, The Blessing and the Curse: The Burning of Wives in India*, Oxford University Press, 1994, pp. 101-130.

published in almanacs and books, which are available everywhere in India. Amazingly, even in our modern scientific age, some religious Hindus use these texts to make important decisions.

For example, in the Bengali month of Magh (approximately December 15 to January 15), and Chitra (approximately March 15 to April 15), many Bengali Hindus do not buy new property or start new businesses. Some Hindu families arrange the date of weddings to fall on special days in certain months in accord with the recommendations of the almanacs. When I first came to the U.S., my mother did not want me to leave Kolkata on September 5, 1980, because it was not an auspicious day. But I left India anyway because the flight was less expensive. Leaving Kolkata on September 5, an inauspicious date, has had no negative impact on my life.

In addition to this list, there are many other superstitions in Hinduism which I do not believe (see Table 3).

As I mentioned earlier, as a Hindu I believe in the ancient teaching of the Vedas, but I am confused as to how the 33 gods and goddesses described in the Rig Veda became 330 million gods and goddesses. I also do not believe in the caste system because in the eyes of God all human beings are equal.

I have lived most of my life as a skeptic. Though sometimes I have thought there must be a loving kind God, for on many occasions I felt his blessings in my life. For example, when I was struggling with my job at the University of Chicago, an opening at the University of New Mexico appeared from nowhere (the person working in the position I wanted decided to retire early). Moreover, when I needed open heart surgery, my kind friends took care of me, and when I was lonely and depressed, God sent my wife Alice to me to complete my life. However, the scientist in me always believed that humans created God, not that God created us. Then in June 2011, my mother came back from death after my Christian wife prayed at her bedside. There is no medical explanation for her survival. God performed a miracle to prove his existence. As a scientist how can I overlook such overt evidence?

I began reading Hindu scriptures, the Bible, and books written on both Hinduism and Christianity, with the love and respect of a believer. I have been lucky to meet gifted spiritual teachers, both in

India and the U.S., and I remember their teachings as well. Eventually I decided that I wanted to share my spiritual journey, from a skeptic to a believer, from Hinduism to Christianity, with the public. I was exposed to Christian teachings when I attended kindergarten at Holy Child School in Calcutta, and I have loved Jesus since I was five years old. As a born Hindu, my spiritual journey starts at Hinduism and ends in Christianity.

According to ancient Hindu scriptures, the name of the supreme God is Brahman, who is eternal and beyond human perception. Brahman existed before the Big Bang, and will continue to exist even after our current universe disappears. Time is eternal and when one universe is destroyed a new universe is created, and this process of creation and destruction repeats in a cyclic manner, with no beginning or end. This philosophy is supported by scientific theory; namely, that when our current universe is destroyed, a new Big Bang will give birth to a new universe. However, for each cycle, Brahman creates Brahma, who is then put in charge of creating all matter in the new universe. Brahma lives for 311 trillion 40 billion years, after which everything in the universe is destroyed due to his death. We are currently living in the 51st Brahma year of the current Brahma, and after another 49 Brahma years (approximately 155 trillion years), our universe will be demolished. (See chapter 7).

Brahman is the supreme God, similar to Jehovah of the Hebrew scriptures and the New Testament. "Jehovah" is mentioned 237 times in The New World Translation of the Holy Scriptures." However, Brahma, the creator of the present universe is not immortal like Jehovah.

In Christianity, faithful people often talk about God (Jehovah or the Lord), who sent his only son Jesus Christ for the salvation of humanity. In contrast, in the modern practice of Hinduism the word "Brahman" is rarely used. Moreover, there is a temple in India which is dedicated to Brahma, but there is no temple for the supreme God Brahman.

Although I mention Brahman several times in this book—so that readers can understand the link between Brahman and Brahma—at the present time the religious/spiritual journey of most Hindus starts with Brahma not the supreme God Brahman. Therefore, I like to think that my spiritual odyssey has taken me from Brahma to Jehovah.

CONCLUSIONS

Hinduism is a religion, but at the same time also a philosophy. Many original Hindu texts are lost, and to those remaining many modifications have been made. For example, only 33 gods and goddesses are described in the Rig-Veda, where Brahman is the supreme God. However, Adi Shankara of the early 8th Century preached the Advaita Vedanta School of philosophy (non-dualism). According to this doctrine, the ultimate God Brahman is the only entity, and the ultimate goal of human life is to dissolve his/her soul in the vastness of Brahman. This is a frightful concept, because if we merge with Brahman (super consciousness), we will no longer retain our individual identity. I would rather go to heaven and obey God's rules and enjoy his eternal love than lose my individuality in order to become part of God.

Jesus, flanked by angels, ascending into heaven, a mystical Christian allegory of spiritual enlightenment.

One of my spiritual teachers in India told me that it is impossible to understand God through knowledge, and therefore it is a fruitless effort; like teaching our cat Thor to read the *New York Times* every morning. The best approach is to practice good karma and help people to the best of our abilities. Moreover, one must be humble no matter how successful he or she is, for God does not like pride. As we take a bath every day to clean our body, prayer is a bath for our soul.

This world is a school, but as various schools offer various trainings and diplomas, different people are assigned different curriculum. If we are kind, selfless, and live by good ethical and moral standards, we can successfully graduate from Earth School. Knowledge of Sanskrit is not a prerequisite to achieving enlightenment. Living a moral life and having a strong faith is all we need to go heaven.

TABLE 1
VARIOUS THEORIES ATTEMPTING
TO EXPLAIN ORIGIN OF RELIGION

• Max Muller (1823-1900) argued that religion originated out of myths and cults, which were based on the personification of natural phenomena (such as sky, sun, mountain, wind, rocks, etc.).
• Herbert Spencer (1820-1903) argued that religion originated from the respect we feel and give to ancestors.
• Sir E. B. Taylor introduced the animistic theory of religion, where it was believed that both animate and inanimate objects (such as stones, rivers, snakes, and lions) have souls.
• Emile Durkheim (1858-1917) argued that religion originated in totemic rites, designed to promote the social solidarity of a given tribe. In totemism each individual is believed to have a spiritual connection or kinship with another specific physical being, such as an animal or plant, called a "spirit-being" or "totem."
• Sigmund Freud (1856-1939), the father of psychoanalysis, considered religion to be an expression of an underlying psychological neurosis and the innate stresses of the human condition.
• According to the Terror Management Theory (TMT) religion is a coping mechanism to deal with the fear of death (which only humans can experience because animals live in the present).
• Karl Marx considered religion "the opiate of the masses."

TABLE 2
MOST COMMONLY MENTIONED
RELIGIOUS TEXTS OF HINDUISM

• The Rig-Veda: This text, the oldest known Hindu religious scripture, originated between 1700-1100 BC, and contains 1071 hymns. In the Rig-Veda 33 deities (gods and goddesses) were mentioned, with most of the hymns dedicated to Indra, king of all divinities. Indian astrology can also be traced back to the Rig-Veda.
• The Sama-Veda, a collection of melodies borrowed from the Rig-Veda (limited new information).
• The Yajur-Veda served as a guidebook to priests who performed Hindu religious ceremonies, including sacrifices.
• The Atharva-Veda is different from other Vedas because it embodies an

independent parallel tradition to that of the Rig-Veda and the Yajur-Veda. It describes early traditions of healing and magic that had parallels in other Indo-European texts. It was also the last of all the Vedas.
- The Ramayana and the Mahabharata are two epics of Hindu religion.
- The Puranas were probably written after the Ramayana and the Mahabharata, but there is much debate regarding the exact time this occurred. The Puranas describe myths surrounding the birth of the universe, and contain stories of ancient kings, as well as gods and goddesses.
- The Bhagavad Gita, or simply Gita, is probably the holiest book of Hinduism. It describes the law of karma and encourages living a life engaging in selfless karma (*nishkam karma*).
- In the 4th Century Patanji wrote the Yoga Sutra, which is the basis of practice of yoga.
- In the 8th Century Adi Shankara preached the philosophy of Advaita Vedanta.

TABLE 3
SOME SUPERSTITIONS OF THE
HINDU RELIGION I DO NOT BELIEVE

- Long distance travel on Saturday and also Thursday noon must be avoided. Saturday is considered to be a very inauspicious day due to its association with the god Shani (Saturn). There is also a particular time each a day called *Rahukaal*, when new jobs should not be initiated.
- No one should get a haircut on Saturday, possibly also on Tuesday or Thursday.
- You must add one rupee to every gift; for example, do not offer a gift of 100 rupees, it must be 101.
- In the Hindu family a menstruating woman is not allowed to go to temple, or even worship at home.
- Avoid marrying a person (especially a woman) born under an inauspicious aspect of the planet Mars (*mangalik*), because her husband will die, fating her to becoming a widow.
- A black cat crossing your path will bring bad luck.
- The new moon day (*Amavasya*) is a very inauspicious day for Hindus. People should not start any new project or buy property.

- An eclipse (both solar and lunar) is considered an inauspicious time by Hindus. People should not go out during an eclipse and probably should not work. All cooked foods must be discarded after the completion of an eclipse.
- In some parts of India Hindus do not sweep their house at night.
- The tail end of a cow is considered its most sacred part.
- East is an auspicious direction and it is recommended that one sleep at night facing east (the head must face east). Never sleep with your head facing north because eventually you will suffer from many diseases.
- Eating yogurt before an exam brings good luck, but avoid eating bananas or eggs.

2

A RELIGIOUS MOTHER & AN ATHEIST FATHER

INTRODUCTION

I was born in a middle class family in Calcutta (now Kolkata), India. Kolkata is the eastern metropolitan city of India where Mother Teresa (1910-1997) spent many years of her life and founded the Missionaries of Charity, a Roman Catholic religious congregation. This charitable organization is credited for many outstanding contributions, including providing hospices for the homeless, homes for patients suffering from AIDS, leprosy, and tuberculosis, orphanages, soup kitchens, dispensaries, and mobile clinics for the poor.

Mother Teresa received the 1979 Nobel Peace Prize, and a year later, "Bharat Ratna," the highest civilian honor in India. Although this honor is usually conferred upon people of Indian origin, in 1990 President Nelson Mandala was the recipient of the award as well. In 2003 Mother Teresa was beatified as "Blessed Teresa of Calcutta" by the Vatican. A second miracle is required for her sainthood.

Kolkata is also the birth place of Rabindranath Tagore, a famous poet, writer, and philosopher, and the only recipient of the Nobel Prize in literature (1913) from the Indian subcontinent, for his book *Gitanjali*. After his win, Tagore founded a school in Shantiniketan (a Bengali word meaning "peaceful home"), which became a university, Visha Bharati, in 1921. Today Visha Bharati is a highly reputed central school in India, with degrees granted in both the liberal arts and science. Many famous people have studied at Visha Bharati, including Indira Gandhi and Professor Amartya Sen, the former prime minister of India and a Nobel Laureate in economics.

Amitava's parents: Mr. Anil Kumar Dasgupta and Mrs. Hasi Dasgupta, in 1995.

Marriage between my mother and father was arranged: they had never met before the wedding day (father was brave to marry a stranger; I cannot imagine putting myself in that situation). Father was an atheist, but my grandparents were devout Hindus. Mother lost her father at a young age and was facing severe financial problems. At the time of her marriage, she was a high school teacher supporting her widowed mother and a younger sister. Why did my grandfather arrange the marriage? When I asked that question he said he felt sorry for her. But the positive aspect was a fine astrological match between the horoscopes of my mother and father.

Many Hindus even today blindly believe in astrology. In one instance my father told me a story where a mother took her young son for an astrological consultation. The astrologer predicted that the son would be counting lots of money every day. His prediction came true, because when the boy grew up he found a job working as a bank teller. Father did not believe in astrology right up to near his death in 2011, when told me that an astrologer can make only one forecast accurately:

his or her client will die one day.

Mother is a dedicated Hindu, and I think my grandparents arranged that marriage with a hope that she would influence my father to finally believe in God one day. She is a devotee of Lord Shiva. My parents went to Puri India for their honeymoon, which is a famous temple dedicated to Lord Jagannath (Lord of the Universe). Puri is about 300 miles from Kolkata, but the view of the Bay of Bengal from Puri is spectacular. Mother told me that I was born because Lord Jagannath blessed her. Father thought differently, for I am neither handsome nor smart.

MY CHILDHOOD AND EARLY ADOLESCENCE

Although mother was an enthusiastic Hindu, she did not object to father's idea to send me to a Christian Missionary school close to our home. Father convinced her that a good background in English is essential to being successful in India, because English is the link-language throughout the country (Hindi is spoken only in Northern India). Moreover, English is the only medium of instruction in college level sciences and engineering courses. In addition, English is also the medium of instruction in all medicals schools and law schools in India, because medical charts are written in English.

I was admitted into kindergarten at Holy Child School at age 5, and studied there until second grade. Therefore, before I learned the Gayatri mantra (a famous Vedic chant which Brahmins should recite at least three times a day), I learned the Lord's Prayer from the Bible: "Our Father, who art in heaven, hallowed be Thy Name, Thy kingdom come . . ." The sisters teaching at the Holy Child School were very respectful towards Hinduism, and no one tried to convert us to Christianity. I felt close to Jesus because he loves children and I learned to sing Christmas carols. "Silent Night" is still my favorite.

After finishing second grade at Holy Child School, father decided to enroll me at Hare School. I eventually completed my high school diploma there. Hare School was founded in 1818 by David Hare, a businessman from Scotland who loved India, and devoted his life to educating children in Calcutta/Kolkata. Hare School is one of the oldest schools in the city. While I was in the eighth grade, I decided that I wanted to focus my curriculum on humanism, because I wanted to be a poet. I was at that time writing poetry and won prizes in several children poetry contests. I expressed my interest to my father and he told me to take a look at my face in the mirror. He then asked me "How do you look?" I told him, "I am not handsome, but not ugly either." He agreed with my assessment and told me to go for a science major.

His logic was that due to the way I look, there was no possibility for me to become a hero in a movie (the only role I could play would be a waiter serving food to the hero and heroin in an Indian restaurant). Moreover, there is no way a beautiful rich woman would fall in love with me and support me. He told me that it would be far easier for me to get a job with a science background, and possibly a woman might marry me one day. I was a teenager and liked all the females around me, regardless of physical appearance. I decided to be a science major so that I might get married one day and legally kiss a woman.

I grew up confused because I was sandwiched between a religious mother and an atheist father. Although my grandparents were committed Hindus, my two uncles who lived with us were both atheists like my father (many families during the 1960s and 1970s in India were joint families, where parents lived with their married sons, daughter-in-laws, and their grandchildren; such traditions are no longer common in urban areas, and today many Indian families living in big cities are nuclear families). However, the atheism of my father and uncles was counterbalanced by my aunts who were religious.

As a child I believed in Hindu gods and goddesses, along with Jesus as our savior. It may appear confusing, but many Hindus accept Jesus as an Avatar (a Sanskrit word meaning "descent of God," which fits with the Christian belief that Jesus is the son of God). Moreover, the image of the crucifixion of Jesus made me cry as a child. I had no doubt that Jesus died on the cross for our wrongdoings, and that his blood washed away all the sins committed by humans in the past, and that it would wash away all of the future sins of mankind.

MY ADOLESCENCE YEARS

Despite my belief in both Jesus and Hindu deities as well, father did not interfere. Probably he waited for the right time. When I was thirteen I asked him why he did not believe in God. He said, "Why don't we do an experiment to see if God listens to our prayers. You pray hard to Lord Shiva, so that your mother will not scold you for the entire week, because your mother is a devotee of Lord Shiva." Unfortunately for me, on the third day of prayer mother screamed at me, indicating that my prayer had failed to yield the desired result.

When I was in high school father explained to me that the universe was created through the Big Bang, and humans came into the world through the path of evolution following Darwin's theory. Later, as an adult, I found out that dad was correct, because genetic evidence, including mitochondrial DNA studies, reveal that modern humans (*Homo sapiens*) originated in sub-Saharan Africa 200,000 years ago (although older forms of humans could be traced back even further to 500,000 years ago).

Moreover, analysis of fossils found in Israel indicate that the earliest human migration out of Africa started from the Kalahari Desert and the African rainforest 90,000 years ago, although most of the migrations took place 55,000-85,000 years ago.

Asia was inhabited first, followed by Australia, which was inhabited 50,000 years ago when a small band of humans arrived there by boats or rafts. However, oceans were less deep at that time compared to current depths. Europe was inhabited last, approximately 27,000 to 16,000 years ago.[22] The latest human migration took place in the Pacific islands; for example, East Polynesia was inhabited only 1000 years ago.[23]

Humans who migrated out of sub-Saharan Africa had brown skin. There are several hypotheses regarding the origin of white skin and the Caucasian race. Interestingly, the word "Caucasian" does not mean white skin, because the word Caucasian race describes physical features of populations of Europe, North Africa, and Mediterranean without regard to skin tone. The skin color of humans depends on the concentration of melanin, a pigment that protects the skin from ultraviolet radiation. White skin has less concentration of melanin than brown or dark skin.

Some scientists have postulated that lighter skin offered a strong

---

22. Nesheva D. "Aspects of ancient mitochondrial DNA analysis in different population for understanding human evolution." Balkan J Med Genet 2014; 17: 5-14.
23. Matisoo-Smith E. "Ancient DNA and the human settlement of the Pacific-a review." J Human Evol 2015; 79: 93-104.

survival advantage to ancient people who migrated from North Africa to Europe by boosting their vitamin D level. Ultraviolet light is needed for the synthesis of vitamin D, which strengthens bones; but a high melanin concentration in the skin blocks ultraviolet light from entering the skin and synthesizing vitamin D. Therefore, vitamin D deficiency is more common in dark skinned people than fair skinned people.

Cheng and his colleagues discovered a genetic mutation in the SLC24A5 gene explaining the origin of white skin. This gene plays an important role in determining one's natural skin color. Europeans carry a variant of this gene (mutation) due to a change in one letter in the DNA code (out of 3.1 billion letters in the human genome), and this genetic mutation is responsible for white skin color. The exact time this mutation took place is hard to pinpoint, but researchers theorize that it probably occurred 20,000 to 50,000 years ago.[24]

The Hindu savior-god Krishna or Chrishna, whose name has the same Indo-European rootword as the Greek *Christos* or Christ: the Chaldean word *chris*, meaning the "sun," the ancient symbol of enlightenment.

When I was an adolescent father convinced me that if there is a God, he lives at the center of our Milky Way Galaxy, which is 30,000 light years from earth. Therefore, it must take 30,000 years for a prayer to reach God (light is the fastest travelling entity in the universe). As soon as God listens to our prayer he grants it, but his approval of our prayer travelling at the speed of light takes another 30,000 years to reach earth. If a human could live for at least 60,000 years, he/she would discover that God truly does grant all of our prayers. Unfortunately, our life span is too short.

When I asked mother her opinion on this she disagreed and said

---

24. Lamason R, Mohideen MA, Mest JR, Wong AC et al. "SLC24A5, a putative cation exchanger, affects pigmentation in Zebrafish and humans." *Science* 2005; 310: 1781-1786.

God is beyond all science and that Lord Shiva hears our prayer as soon as we utter it. For example, "I prayed for your dad's promotion and he got it," she told me once. "Maybe he received a promotion because of his hard work," I replied. Mother got angry and said that "without God's approval nothing is possible in this world." Why then did God "approve" of the killing of millions of innocent people by Hitler and his gangs?

This time mother had no good answer and she told me to shut up. Father told me that when questioned this is the common religious response when defending God—even though his actions are clearly irrational in some cases.

MY HIGH SCHOOL GRADUATION

Although I am an only child, my mother did not use "family planning" when it came to the number of Hindu gods and goddesses she had in her home shrine. Whenever she heard about the glory of a new deity from another devotee, she simply adopted it.

In India every state has a board of secondary education and every student must take a set of comprehensive examinations lasting for one to two weeks in order to graduate from high school. A particular school authority has no right to issue a diploma. Although I attended Hare School, my high school diploma was issued by the West-Bengal Broad of Secondary Education. Passing the high school comprehensive exam is a big deal because the names and pictures of the top ten students are published in the newspapers, even today. Moreover, the top 100 students are selected to receive a "National Scholarship" and students who are placed in the highest passing grades (first division) can get admission to elite colleges and universities.

Mother, being a high school teacher, was hoping that I would place in the top ten students, and she started praying hard to all the gods and goddesses known to the Hindu religion. Her morning prayers were so loud that I did not need an alarm clock to wake up in the morning. Father begged her to lower her voice a little (once he told me that some Hindu gods, due to advanced age, might need hearing aids) so that he could sleep a little longer. But it did not work.

Mother encouraged me to start praying, but father convinced me that Lord Shiva could not take the exam for me, so it would be best for me to study hard instead of praying. My grandparents were on mother's side, but my dad and uncles convinced me that hard work is the one and only key to success.

I still remember April 16, 1975, when the results of the West Bengal Board of Secondary Education examination were officially announced for the year. At that time there were no home computers, so the board published a gazette with the names, total marks in all subjects, and the passing grades (there are three passing grades: first division, equivalent to A, second division, and third division) of all the successful students. No reporter showed up at our apartment, which meant that I had not placed in the list of the top 10 students. Mother was very upset, but I was not disappointed at all.

I went to my high school to see my total score. Mother told me not to commit suicide if my name was not published in the gazette (the names of the unsuccessful students are not printed in the paper). I found out that I passed in the first division with decent marks—which was what I had expected. Unfortunately, no one from our high school was in the top 10, and our principal was very upset and blamed me for not studying hard enough.

I returned to our house and found that father had come home a little early from work. He was happy with my result and hoped my name would be in the merit list (top 100 students). Mother was still angry and said my poor performance was due to my atheism. My next door neighbor, hearing mother's scream, came to our apartment and told her that I was young and that I would certainly pass next year. My offended mother told our neighbor my score. She was delighted and asked me to come to her apartment so that she could give me some Indian sweets as a congratulatory gesture.

Mother was still fuming, so dad finally intervened. He said it was jealousy: I had outperformed mom, because she had placed only in the second division in her high school examination. That only made her more upset, so I decided to leave her alone.

Fortunately when the merit list was published I was in the top 100 students, which earned me a national scholarship. I told mother that Lord Shiva, despite not praying to him, was not angry, because if he really had been I would have failed the exam. She claimed her devotion rescued me from disaster, and it was due only to her prayer that I managed to get my name on the merit list.

MY SPIRITUAL JOURNEY AS YOUNG ADULT

I enrolled at the Presidency College affiliated with Calcutta University in 1975 with a major in chemistry. My goal at the time was to obtain my Bachelor's degree and then to study for a Master's degree and, if very fortunate, to obtain a Ph.D. so that I could be a college professor one day. At the time I continued my creative writing, focusing on poetry.

In 1975 I met two important people, both spiritual and both professors. Professor Banerjee taught philosophy in a college and he moved to our neighborhood that year. Professor Chatterjee was teaching botany. I met him through a friend Pramila, who was his student. Apart from being a professor of botany, he was also a master astrologer and palmist. When we first met he accurately told my past, but I thought he had done his homework by asking Pramila. When I challenged him he told me that I was a very sick child, which Pramila did not know. Later, my relation with him warmed up and I started calling him "Deepak Babu." (In Bengali culture adding "Babu" after the first name is customary if one wants to show respect to an elder or an esteemed person. It is similar to calling someone "sir.")

Though the practices of astrology and astronomy had common roots, Sir Isaac Newton (1642-1727) united astronomy with the laws of mechanics (physics), after which astrology was separated from astronomy. Astronomers examine the positions, motions, and properties of celestial objects, while an astrologer attempts to predict future events in people's lives based on the positions and transits of the planets. Therefore astrology is not a science, because it is impossible for planets to affect different individuals differently.

Moreover, if Saturn, which is 890 million miles from earth, has such a profound effect on humans, then why do low orbit artificial satellites, which are only 300-500 miles away from earth, have no effect on humans? In addition, in Western astrology planets that were discovered much later, such as Neptune, Uranus and Pluto, are also placed in one's horoscope, and these planets, depending on their position, also render various effects.

For example, in astro-cartography (also called astro-geography, invented by American astrologer Jim Lewis, 1941-1995) a person is advised not to live in a place where the Pluto line passes through the astro-cartography chart, because living on the Pluto line can be difficult; but if the Jupiter line passes through the chart it is a desirable location to live. In Indian astrology, however, planets such as Uranus, Neptune and Pluto, are not included. Therefore Western astrology must be more advanced than India astrology because three more planets are included in one's horoscope.

At that point Deepak Babu told me that neither palmistry nor astrology should be considered a science because two people with very similar astrological charts may have different life paths. In order to be a good astrologer or palmist, a psychic gift is essential. A psychic is born not made.

For some reason Deepak Babu attracted me like a magnet. Although I never took a botany class, I often visited him just to chat. He lived alone and he also liked me.

One day I asked him about intuition and he told me that the vision of science is limited, and that there are other universes which are beyond the reach of current astronomical observations. He was also well versed in physics and told me about dark energy and parallel universes. I told him that I sometimes see or feel future events. He said that I have intuition and that I should develop it.

He began to teach me palmistry. One day I asked him about certain lines on my palm which indicate that I would live and die in a foreign country. Intuitively he felt that this was true, and that the foreign country would most likely be the U.S. However, sending me to the U.S. for higher study was completely beyond the financial reach of my parents at the time. He told me that he and I should go for a consultation with the great psychic Bistu Babu, who lived in a small town 30 miles from Kolkata. To make sure we got an appointment we were to take the first train at 4:30 AM.

SEEING BISTU BABU

One cold morning in January 1976, Deepak Babu and I started our journey at 4 AM for the local train station. We arrived at Bistu Babu's very old house around 5:30 AM, and at 6:30 AM he called me for my consultation. Deepak Babu came with me.

My reading was brief. Bistu Babu looked at my palm for few seconds and then looked at me and said, "You won't like what I am going to tell you, but this is your destiny. You will go to the U.S. in 1980 then change your career, as I see you as a professor in a medical school doing both research and clinical service. Later in life you will write many books and will experience much spiritual growth. You will marry late to a white professional woman who wears glasses. Her hair will be light in color, possibly blonde or red, and her first name will start with the letter A."

I was very upset as my ideal woman at that time was an Indian woman with long black hair. Bistu Babu looked at me and said, "Don't try to beat your destiny, but since you do not like my reading please do not give me any donation." Nonetheless, I gave him five Indian rupees (approximately 10 cents).

Deepak Babu finally opened his mouth and said, "Thank you so much, because I gave a similar reading to Amitava based on the lines on his palm. Now I am convinced that his destiny is in the U.S., and I will guide him in the right direction."

We left Bistu Babu's house and Deepak Babu told me not to worry about the reading, but for the time being to focus on my studies. I told mother about Bistu Babu and she took me to a different astrologer, who assured her that I would stay in India and marry an Indian woman. But this prediction would only come true if she spent 5000 Indian rupees so that he could do a special ritual to circumvent the ill effects of "Kalsarpa Yoga," a very bad planetary arrangement in my horoscope.

Father intervened and convinced mother not to waste any money, and also told her that getting an American education would make me more marketable in India for an academic job. Father also assured mom that due to the way I look, a blonde American woman would never want to date me. However, he instructed mother to continue to pray hard to Lord Shiva, just in case a crazy blonde or red-haired woman showed an interest.

In order to test Bistu Babu's psychic gift my mother took my aunt (mom's sister) for a reading, and I went as their guide to help find the house. Mom entered Bistu Babu's chamber for the reading, along with my aunt, and both came back angry after half an hour. Bistu Babu told mother that she would not be able to prevent me from going to the U.S. and marrying an American woman. He also advised my aunt not to get married because her destiny was to be a widow. Her husband would not live for more than four years after marrying her, and nothing could be done astrologically to prevent the tragedy.

My mother and aunt concluded that Bistu Babu must be a fraud, and later, when my aunt consulted another astrologer, he told her that her widowhood could be prevented by performing a costly ritual after her marriage.

Mother came home and for the first time in my life encouraged me to date. However, prior to going to Bistu Babu she criticized every woman who came to our house. One was not good looking; another did not dress modestly because she wore a short skirt showing her legs, etc. But after listening to Bistu Babu she seems to have decided that it would be better for me to look at the legs of an Indian woman than an American woman.

Just to tease mother, father advised me to marry an American woman because mom would not be able to pick a fight with her daughter-in-law due to her poor English. But this only infuriated mother. I decided there and then to study hard instead of looking for a girlfriend, because my scholarship was only 150 Indian rupees and I did not want to borrow money from my parents for dating.

MEETING PROFESSOR BANERJEE

In 1975 I met Professor Banerjee, who had moved to our neighborhood. He was a confirmed bachelor who lived with his aunt, a confirmed bachelorette. Professor Banerjee dwelt in a different reality and spent most of his time studying both Indian and Western philosophy.

My mother, who taught Sanskrit in a high school, also taught Sanskrit to me with the hope that one day I would be interested in reading the Gita, the holy Indian text. But instead, because my hormones were raging, I was interested in reading Sanskrit poetic literature, some of which contained erotica. One such book was the *Kumar Sambhava* by Kalidasa, which provides a detailed description of the love-making between Lord Shiva and his wife Parvati.

Professor Banerjee was spiritual but not religious. He told me how modern Hinduism has deviated from the original teachings of the Vedas and the Bhagavad Gita, to a modern, complex mixture of paganism and henotheism (a belief in one supreme God along with many additional gods and goddesses, also known as demigods and

Amitava with his parents in New York City in 2000, with the World Trade Center in the background.

demigoddesses). And although he was a Brahmin (the highest caste), he rejected the caste system. This is because the caste system in ancient India was simply a division of labor, not a class system—which is what it became later. Moreover, in the original system a person born in a lower caste could move to a higher caste based on education, religious practice, and the display of high moral values that were similar to Brahmins. Unfortunately, Professor Banerjee passed away in 2002. I still miss him.

Professor Banerjee once explained to me how horrible some Hindu rituals are, such as sati (widow-burning), which began "polluting" the Hindu religion around 17th Century. As discussed earlier, the entire purpose of this hideous rite was to deny widows the rightful inheritance of their husbands' property.

TEACHINGS OF PROFESSOR BANERJEE

Professor Banerjee also taught me the Indian version of dialectic materialism. Rishi Charvak (*Rishi* in Sanskrit means "saint") introduced the Lokayata philosophy, which states that there is nothing beyond this material world (*Lok*) and at death human existence comes to an end, for there is no God and no soul. He also taught me the Samkhya philosophy (professed by Kapil Muni), a good Indian example of metaphysical dualism; but unlike many of its Western counterparts it is atheistic in nature.

Samkhya philosophy describes the presence of two realities in the universe: *prakriti* ("matter" or nature) and *purusha* ("self" or spirit). Prakriti is comprised of three gunas or qualities: 1. *sattva guna* (noble and spiritual qualities); 2. *rajas guna* (hard work and a passion for life); and

3. *tamas guna* (darkness or a materialistic approach to life). Both purusha and prakriti are eternal and independent of each other. Creation is due to the interaction between purusha and prakriti. There is no God in this philosophy, making it an atheistic school of thought.

Professor Banerjee also introduced the principles of Tantra to me. Tantra has long been one of the most neglected branches of Indian spiritual studies, despite the existence of many ancient books written between the 5th and 9th Centuries discussing in detail how to practice Tantra in order to experience enlightenment.

Tantric philosophy is based on Vedic philosophy, but it represents the practical aspect of the Vedic tradition. The main god in Tantra is Lord Shiva and the main goddess is his wife Parvati, also known as Shakti (in Sanskrit this word literally means "energy"). Shakti is also known as a mother-goddess, a goddess of love, and a goddess of fertility and devotion.

According to Tantra our universe was created due to the union of Lord Shiva and Parvati. One aspect of Tantra is that anyone, regardless of caste, can learn and practice Tantra for spiritual growth, while the study of the Vedas in ancient India was restricted to Brahmins only. In addition, women are placed above men in Tantra because the universe is run by Shakti, and only Shakti can mobilize male energy (which is inactive) in a positive and creative way.

Tantra is a practical manual that provides step by step instructions by which an ordinary man, who is at the level of animal consciousness, can uplift his consciousness to the level of a god. However, Tantra does not ignore the lower bodily needs, such as sex, but gives advice on how to keep one's sexual needs under control.

Tantric practices include tantric meditation, which can transform sexual energy into spiritual energy by awaking the "Kundalini," represented by Shakti, or sometimes a coiled snake, centered at the base of the spine.[25] When Kundalini is activated by the tantric method, and the sleeping serpent is "awakened," or as Jesus phrased it, "lifted up,"[26]

---

25. It is this Hindu reptile which entered Hebrew mythology as the "serpent" who tempted Eve in the Garden of Eden. Lochlainn Seabrook. *The Way of Holiness: The Story of Religion and Myth, From the Cave Bear Cult to Christianity*, Vol. 1 Sea Raven Press, unpublished manuscript.
26. John 3:14-15.

Kundalini energy winds up through the spine to unite with Lord Shiva, her lover, located at the crown chakra at the top of the head. When this spiritual love making takes place (known in both the ancient Graceo-Roman mystery religions and Gnostic Christianity as the *Hieros Gamos*, or "Sacred Union"),[27] the practitioner (that is, the tantric) experiences enlightenment and can break away from the cycle of birth and death.

Unfortunately in the West, the *spiritual* love making between Shakti and Lord Shiva has been misinterpreted, giving Tantra a negative reputation, as if it were a sex manual like the Kama Sutra. It is important to remember that the Kama Sutra is a book which teaches couples how to get the best out of love making. The Kama Sutra is not a holy text. In contrast, the principles of Tantra are based on Vedic philosophy, and tantric practice is a practical spiritual path to enlightenment. A true tantric sees the reflection of the Mother-Goddess in every woman and has complete control over his sexuality.

In the text of Tantra there is mention of "holy spiritual union," where a man during intercourse with a female (Shakti) is not allowed to ejaculate, and this is the ultimate test to see if his mind can control his body. According to Tantra, during the spiritual lovemaking session, instead of ejaculation, seminal fluid containing sperm travels upwards through the spine, and this movement is called *urdhvareta* (literally, the "upward flow of sexual fluids") in Sanskrit.[28] My teacher told me that this is actually the ascending movement of the Kundalini energy from the base chakra to the crown chakra, after which it unites with the male energy (Shiva). After spiritual union the tantric is enlightened and acquires all knowledge of the universe as well as every other realm.

Although a tantric is allowed to try this (which is the most difficult tantric practice) with any willing woman, my teacher informed me that no tantric in India would ever dare practice this ritual with anyone other than his spouse. This is because a tantric who ejaculates during holy intercourse may lose all of his good karma.

According to Tantra the human body has seven chakras (energy points) with the base chakra located near the tailbone at the end of the

---

27. Lochlainn Seabrook. *Christmas Before Christianity: How the Birthday of the "Sun" Became the Birthday of the "Son."* Sea Raven Press, 2010, pp. 53, 160, 168, 176, 196.
28. It is also spelled urdhva-reta and urdhva reta.

spine, and the highest chakra, the crown chakra, at the top of the head. Therefore, during chakra alignment, a practitioner may need to touch his/her client. This is similar to the type of massage practiced by a licensed massage therapist—except that chakra balancing does not require a state license. A gifted Reiki Master can also perform chakra balancing using a client's energy field (as well as stones and crystals) without touching him or her. Therefore, one can lie on a massage table or bed fully clothed.

Ultimately, tantric sex and tantric massage are the creations of Westerners, not Indians.

COMING TO THE U.S.

I studied hard during my undergraduate years and my grades were good. As I was nearing graduation, Deepak Babu reminded me of the reading of Bistu Babu from January 1976. My astrological chart indicates that I would spend most of my life in a foreign land. Moreover, according to numerology my birth number is 7. Although 7 provides a good spiritual vibration and is the number of the union of male and female energies,[29] it can also be the number of loneliness. As a result, at that time I concluded that I might live alone in the U.S. for part or even the rest of my life. I was not excited about this at all.

I graduated with the highest passing grade (first class) and Deepak Babu advised me to take the GRE exam. I reluctantly agreed.

There was a center for taking the test in Kolkata, but my mother was not happy about my intention to take it. When the examination score came to our home address (I was then living with my parents), she opened the letter, but was not familiar with the percentile system. Father convinced her that I had performed very poorly, because the 99th percentile meant that 99 percent of all exam takers performed better than me.

When I came home after soccer practice, mother told me about my poor GRE performance. Although she was happy about it, she pretended to be sad. Father took me for a walk and when we were at a

---

29. The Masculine Principle is symbolized by the number three, while the Feminine Principle is symbolized by the number four, which, when added together, equals seven. Lochlainn Seabrook. *The Way of Holiness: The Story of Religion and Myth, From the Cave Bear Cult to Christianity.* Sea Raven Press, unpublished manuscript.

safe distance from home, he explained to me that it would be another six months before I could go to the U.S., and for this reason he did not want to upset mother now.

He also advised me to enroll in the Master's Program at Calcutta University, but at the same I should apply to different U.S. schools. Although I was rejected by Harvard and Yale, I was fortunate enough to get admission and full financial aid at the University of Georgia at Athens, and decided to accept the offer. At that time my plan was to go to the U.S. and then return to India after completing my Ph.D. degree.

FLYING TO THE U.S.

Father, being a government official in a high position, managed to get my passport without police verification (in order to get a passport in India, official verification is important: a police officer not only checks for a criminal record, but also comes to the applicant's home to interview him/her personally).

One day I went to the U.S. consulate nearby to get my student visa. At that point father bought my plane ticket and told mother. She was very disconcerted, and after 23 years of marriage, realized that she had made a mistake marrying my father, a cold-hearted human being. Father explained to her that it might be too late to get a divorce and that going to the U.S. would be a good move for me. Mother remembered Bistu Babu's prediction, but father assured her that I would not have the guts to date a blonde woman, because my relationship track record in India was a straight F grade.

One Indian woman I liked in my class told me that she would rather be single for the rest of her life than fall in love with me. Another woman liked me a lot, but more like a baby brother. Dad told mom that the only way I would ever get married would be through an arranged marriage. He also convinced her that my market value for arranging a marriage would be greatly improved if I had an American degree.

I left India September 5, 1980, taking a British Airways flight to London connecting to New York, and then flying to Atlanta. Leaving Kolkata was scary because I did not know anyone in the U.S. Deepak Babu came to the airport to see me off and assured me that according to my astrological chart, I would be luckier in the U.S. than in India, and that I would soon have several caring American friends. As it turns out, he was correct.

CONCLUSION

When I returned to India after the completion of my Master's degree in 1981, father explained to me how my original flight plan to the U.S. in September 1980 had come about.

He had paid more money to buy a British Airways ticket because that flight flew non-stop from Kolkata to London. He could have bought a ticket on Air-India at a much lower price, but that flight was scheduled to stop at New Delhi before going onto New York. Father thought I might be too afraid to fly to New York after landing at New Delhi, and instead of flying to the Big Apple, I might get scared and take a flight back to Kolkata. I told father that this was a wise decision, because I had been paralyzed with fear after the British Airways flight took off from Kolkata. I also panicked when my flight landed at London. But by then the initial shock was over and I was able to continue on with my journey.

Amazingly, all of Bistu Babu's predictions came true.

After the completion of my Ph.D. at Stanford University, I switched my field of study to laboratory medicine, with the intention of becoming a toxicologist. I enrolled in a program at the department of Laboratory Medicine at the University of Washington School of Medicine, Seattle, Washington.

My aunt got married in October 1980, and performed the costly ritual recommend by the astrologer to avoid becoming a widow. However, in May 1984, before the end of the fourth year of her marriage, her husband died suddenly from a massive heart attack. She is living her life as a widow as predicted by Bistu Babu, and did not remarry.

After many ups and downs in my life, on February 29, 1996, I met Alice, a red-haired professional woman wearing glasses, who worked in the Federal Court. Three years later, on June 26, 1999, we got married. Today we live in Houston, where I am employed as a Professor of Pathology and Laboratory Medicine at the University of Texas Medical School at Houston.

But I am getting ahead of myself.

3

LIFE IN THE UNITED STATES OF AMERICA

INTRODUCTION

I arrived in Athens, Georgia, on September 6, 1980. Coming to the U.S. was effortless because I did not have to fly the plane. It was adjusting to my new life that was not easy. Fortunately at the University of Georgia I came in contact with a very helpful Indian student, Balkrishna, who arranged for me to share an apartment with another Indian student. He also taught me a simple way of cooking Indian food, as well as basic American manners that would help me adapt to my new life.

For example, I never used deodorant when I lived in India. In the summer months when I took non-air conditioned city buses to go to college, I used to smell like a goat. But everyone else smelled like me, except women who used perfume. Balkrishna told me to use deodorant, and even went to the store with me to show me the right brand to buy.

TROUBLE WITH BRITISH ENGLISH

One week after I arrived at Athens, Georgia, our fall quarter started. I had some trouble understanding the American accent, but I found it even more difficult learning to comprehend American conversational English.

In the first week of my session it was raining and my muffler (the British English word for "scarf") got wet. I went to a department store to buy a new one, but the lady at the counter told me that they did not sell "mufflers," and advised me to go a car repair shop on the next block. However, I saw some nice mufflers in the store, but assumed that cheaper ones might only be available at a car repair shop.

When I went to the car repair shop and asked about purchasing a muffler, the person at the counter asked to see my car. I told him that being a graduate student I could not afford a car, but my muffler got wet due to yesterday's rain. "A wet muffler?" He started laughing loudly, and the other individuals working in the shop also gathered to find out the origin of my "wet muffler."

I explained to him, using gestures, how my muffler got wet. After laughing for at least 10 minutes, he told me that I should go to a department store if I wanted to buy a scarf. In American English a muffler is the silencer on a car's exhaust system, and this kind of a muffler does not get damaged by rain. I went back to the department store and bought a white scarf. When the lady at the store asked me about the muffler, I told her that the car repair shop would take care of it.

Jesus raising the daughter of Jairus from the dead. As always, Jesus refused to take credit for the "miracle," but instead attributed it to Jairus' faith. "Fear not: believe only, and she shall be made whole," he had told the grieving father before the ceremony began. It worked.

I related my story to Balkrishana and he taught me some American vocabulary. For example, in British English rubber means "eraser," but I should not use that word in the U.S. In particular, if I forgot to bring an eraser to class, I should never ask a female student for a rubber. I would certainly get in trouble.

Within a month I learned enough American English to get by and began focusing on my studies. Fortunately, the two blonde women in my class had steady boyfriends, so I stayed out of trouble—despite Bistu Babu's prediction that I would marry a woman with light hair color.

MY FIRST EXPERIENCE OF EATING BEEF

I was studying hard for finals and stopped cooking for a few days. One Sunday evening while walking through downtown Athens I was feeling hungry. I stopped at a McDonald's restaurant and ordered a hamburger with fries and a coca cola. As a Hindu I am allowed to eat pork but not beef, and I thought hamburger must contain ham as the name suggested. I enjoyed the tasty hamburger and went back to my apartment to focus on studying for finals.

After the exams were over, one day I told Balkrishna that I really enjoyed eating a hamburger. He said that he also liked hamburgers and some other American foods, for example, beef stake. Surprised, I asked him, "You eat beef, even though you're a Hindu Brahmin?" He told me that hamburger contains beef. He assured me that God is busy with many important things and does not care if a Hindu eats beef.

GOD DID NOT PUNISH ME

I was worried about receiving some kind of supernatural punishment for eating beef. I could not share my concern with my mother because she might contemplate committing suicide due to my terrible sin. I was preparing myself to get bad grades as a result of my poor decision. Out of desperation I called my father. He assured me that cows in India are holy, but American cows are not. Therefore, eating beef in the U.S. is okay, and Lord Shiva would not manipulate Christian beef-eating professors at the University of Georgia to punish me for eating it.

Two days after eating the hamburger our grades were posted. Fortunately, mine were good. I was relieved and started research for my Master's thesis.

In January 1981 I was feeling more adventurous and contemplated applying to elite schools for a Ph.D. program. I talked to my research guide and he encouraged me to apply to top ranking schools. I applied to Harvard, Stanford, Northwestern, Yale, and few other schools. In the first week of March, I received a nice rejection letter from Harvard. The chair of the admission committee was very sorry because he could not offer me a spot.

A week later Northwestern wanted one more recommendation letter and it looked like they might offer me admission. I was ambitious and called the admission committee chair at Stanford University collect due to my poor financial condition. Professor Huestis told me that the admission committee would meet soon, and I should know the final outcome within the next 10 days. I asked her politely when I should call her again—collect, of course. But she replied that she would call *me*, even if I did not get a spot.

The power of begging paid off. Dr. Huestis phoned a week later offering me admission, and I accepted the offer. She politely reminded me not to call her or any other faculties collect in the near future, or for the rest of my life.

I was now convinced that Lord Shiva was not upset that I ate beef. In fact I was starting to think that eating beef might be bringing me good luck, because the day before Professor Huestis called with the good news, I had eaten a hamburger for lunch.

MOVING TO PALO ALTO

One of the conditions of admission to Stanford was completion of a Master's degree from the University of Georgia prior to formal enrollment. My research guide was very happy, but also told me to work extremely hard so that I could graduate by the summer quarter.

I stopped cooking to save time and started eating at the university cafeteria. Changing food habits was initially difficult because for the first few days I chewed and swallowed my food with the aid of coca cola. However, within a week I started liking American food.

My research professor went out of his way to help me, and I graduated in August, while the fall quarter at Stanford was scheduled to start in late September.

I borrowed money from Balkrishna and went to India for a month. When I landed in Kolkata my mother wanted to know if I had dated any women. I assured her that no one was interested in me, and that I had lived like a monk during my one year stay in Athens. The relief on her face was plain to see.

I left Kolkata again on September 18, 1981, and flew to San Francisco. Fall quarter started soon and for the first time in my life I struggled with my studies. Everyone in my class was brighter than me, and I realized that I am not that smart. Luckily I passed the qualifying exams for my Ph.D., and despite having a B grade in the first quarter,

Professor Carl Djerassi—who discovered oral contraceptives, along with many other contributions to science—accepted me as his graduate student. I did not want to miss out on this opportunity and started studying as diligently as possible.

In my second year I rented a room from a very nice family who lived on Mayfield Avenue. I stayed with them for the rest of my time at Stanford and they were very supportive.

During my third year at Stanford my uncle (my mom's sister's husband) died suddenly from a heart attack. Mother started to believe in the psychic power of Bistu Babu, because my aunt had, as he had predicted, only remained married for three and half-years. When I went back home, for the first time mother did not insist that after getting my Ph.D., I should take the first available flight to return to India.

Eventually, I managed to get my doctorate from Stanford, but at that time I was attracted to the medical sciences and I enrolled in a program at the Department of Laboratory Medicine, University of Washington Medical School at Seattle. I persevered with my studies and after completion of the program I started my first job as Assistant Professor of Pathology at the University of Chicago.

MOVING TO ALBUQUERQUE, NEW MEXICO

I only focused on homework and survival during my days at Stanford and at the University of Washington, but I have to admit that my days at the University of Washington were more enjoyable. However, I grew very little spiritually. At Stanford I briefly met a woman who was proficient in Tantra and she taught me some new chakra balancing techniques and a few other things. However, at the University of Chicago my focus was to get tenure.

In 1989 my parents came to the U.S. for the first time to visit me. Mother wanted me to find a wife, but unfortunately love is not sold in supermarkets. She wanted to put an advertisement for a mate in the *India Abroad* newspaper, but I told her that I should at least get my green card before getting married.

I invited a few friends for dinner so that they could enjoy Indian food. I also invited my boss Dr. Shaw and his wife. Dr. Shaw was very pleased with my mother's cooking and invited us to his home. When we went there for dinner, mom felt very comfortable with the couple and asked them to help her find a girlfriend for me. I was happy that Dr. Shaw did not fire me.

After four years I realized that my academic achievements were way short of the requirements for tenure in an elite school like the University of Chicago, and that it would be better to get out before being kicked out. It reminded me of an experience I had when I was at Stanford and was a teaching assistant for an undergraduate class.

There was a beautiful girl in the class and I was her TA. I never asked her out knowing she would not be interested. After the quarter was over, I saw her at a cafeteria and she asked me why I never asked her out. I told her that I did not want to waste fifty dollars for a date because I was on a tight budget. She had a bet with her friend that I would certainly ask her for a date, as everyone was crazy about her. I told her that if she would pay for the date I would go out with her, so that she could win the bet. She picked me up and took me out to a nice dinner and even a movie, paying for the whole thing. I loved my free date, but never explored a relationship with her because it mostly likely would have ended in failure.

Similarly, tenure at the University of Chicago was completely out of my reach. I thought it would be better to get out before it was denied me and I was labeled a "University of Chicago reject." Moreover, Dr. Shaw, who had gone out of his way to help me with my career, was planning to leave the university. Therefore, my best bet was to seek employment elsewhere.

I saw an opening at the University of New Mexico at Albuquerque and applied. Two months later they called me for an interview. I loved Albuquerque at first sight and my inner voice was telling me I would get an offer. And I did.

My interview went well and I was accepted. I moved to Albuquerque in September 1993 and started working. I also started enjoying life by going for long distance drives on weekends. Albuquerque is full of New Age people and I met Faith, a massage therapist and also a counselor. She was very proficient in energy work and chakra balancing, and I learned a lot from her.

Unfortunately, I had a hard time adjusting to the high altitude and complained about being out of breath. My physician ordered an echocardiogram, and for the first time I found out that I have a birth defect called atrial septal defect (ASD). In normal people the atria are separated by a dividing wall, the interatrial septum. However, if the septum is defective (in my case due to the presence of a big hole), blood flows between the atria (upper chambers) of the heart. As a result, oxygen rich blood mixes with oxygen poor blood. This can lead to lower-than-normal oxygen levels in the arterial blood, which supplies oxygen in the brain and other organs. If the hole is small no surgical intervention is needed. But in my case surgical correction was recommended by the cardiologist.

Atrial septal defect, if significant, increases the risk of developing pulmonary vascular disease, a potentially lethal complication. The risks increase with age, significantly reducing life expectancy. However, surgical correction before age 25 is associated with normal life expectancy.[30] Although I was 35 at the time, the surgeon assured me that I would have a normal life span.

I was scared because I had just started to make new friends and did not yet have a girlfriend. I was not worried about the surgery, but about my post-surgical care. My colleague William Thompson felt bad for me, and told his wife Krista about my situation. She volunteered to help out, as did Marilyn, a medical technologist in our clinical laboratory.

Marilyn invited me to her home and told me that she had a psychic gift. She told me that this surgery was needed to burn some past residual karma I had acquired long before when I threw gladiators into the ring to fight with lions during the time of Roman emperors. Through many reincarnations I had paid for most of my sins. But this residual karma would have to be incinerated by undergoing a major surgery so that my soul could go to the next level. She also predicted that after surgery I would meet my future wife.

Illness and suffering, however, are not always due to bad karma. Sometimes sicknesses help us to better understand mortality, and serve as a spiritual wake up call, forcing us to sort out our priorities. Some individuals have very little residual karma and they may die at a young age from an accident or malady. The law of karma is very complex and

---

30. Geva T, Martins JD, Wald RM. "Atrial septal defect." *Lancet* 383 (9932): 1921-1932.

not always easy to understand.

The surgery was scheduled for May 2, 1994. I decided not to let my parents know because mother is always worried about everything anyway. She is afraid of God, ghosts, dogs, cats and many other things.

When I was young she took me to get a health checkup, where she made the doctor miserable by asking him a million questions. Once she requested that our family physician draw my blood instead of allowing his nurse to draw it, because she had heard that a person can die during the procedure.

When I was a teenager our family physician stopped me one day and told me that if I ever felt ill, to come and see him *without* my mother. Because I was a boy, I told him that I would not be able to pay him. He said that he would rather treat me for free than deal with my mother. From then on I went to see him *gratis*. Once father offered to pay for my visits, but the doctor refused, saying that I was like his child. I was very sad when he passed away.

I knew if I told mother about the surgery she probably would have a heart attack. Even if she could come to the U.S. with father, after seeing me in the ICU post-surgery, she most likely would have fainted. Marilyn told me that there was no need for my parents to come. I stayed with her the day before my surgery and she performed energy work on me. The next morning she drove me to the hospital and I had my operation, during which I had a nice out-of-body experience or OBE.

As Marilyn predicted, I was released from the hospital after five days and she took time off to help me as I recuperated in her house. I made a speedy recovery and went back to work after two weeks. My surgeon and everyone else were surprised, but I knew Marilyn's spiritual healing methods played a part in my recovery.

At that time another woman, Debbie, who was also working in our laboratory as a supervisor, helped me. After recuperation I went back to my apartment and was able to live on my own again, but I was not able to drive for another four weeks. During that period every morning William picked me up as he also worked at the same hospital, and after work I went to his home for dinner. Krista cooked for me for the entire month, and many days she drove me to my apartment. I was able to overcome a big hurdle in my life thanks to my very kind friends.

Two months after surgery I went back to India for a visit and told my parents about the operation. Mother started crying, but father thought my decision of not informing them was correct. My journey home went well, but during my next trip mother pushed me to get married. She even wondered if I might be gay. It was at this time, as Marilyn foretold, that I met my future wife Alice through a common friend. The date was February 29, 1996. I told mother about her, who was utterly relieved to know that I was not a homosexual.

Alice is a good cook and started making meals for me after a few dates at a local Indian restaurant. The first few visits to her house, I took ice cream or chocolate with me; but after that I showed up empty handed for her superb home cooked meals.

MY EXPERIENCE WITH NEW AGE PEOPLE IN ALBUQUERQUE

Albuquerque is one of the great centers of New Age people. I had never encountered so many psychics, astrologers, energy workers, spiritual counselors, etc., in one city before. Out of curiosity I got readings from several psychics, but most had no gift.

Ancient images of the Hindu virgin-mother-goddess Devaki suckling her savior-son Chrishna suffused with Egyptian images of Isis suckling her son, the savior Horus, both born at the Winter Solstice. Much later both were assimilated into Christian depictions of the Virgin-Mary nursing the baby Jesus.

Anyone can use commonsense to make psychic predictions. I have a simple algorithm. Anyone who comes for a psychic reading (usually more women than men) is most likely to have a problem involving either a job or a relationship. Therefore, one's opening statement should be something like this: "I know you are going through a tough time, but always remember God (or Jesus) loves you." In most cases a person will provide bits of revelatory information, such as "my boyfriend is so mean," and then the psychic can say: "He does not deserve a kind nice woman like you. Someone better will show up soon." If the woman is pretty then it is safe to predict that she will have a new boyfriend in less than three months; if not so pretty the time line can be extended to six months or a year.

One finds a similar situation when predicting the time line for acquiring a new job. If the client is highly educated, but lost his/her job due to office politics (it is safe to say you are highly qualified, but your boss is jealous of your popularity), then he/she will find a better job within one to two months. If not so qualified, this should be extended to six months.

Some psychics, without having any gift, simply use logic for a reading. I remember one of my Indian friends at Stanford who, just for fun, did a reading and correctly told a beautiful young woman (a freshmen) that she got two B grades last quarter due to spending too much time with her boyfriend, and that her father was very angry. Later, he said to me that he had made those predictions based on logic. The young woman being attractive most likely had a boyfriend. Therefore, she did not study hard and got two B grades, and thus her father, spending good money for her tuition, would be upset. However, he admitted that predicting the two B grades was a lucky coincidence.

In my opinion a true psychic is born with natural intuition and some individuals are significantly more intuitive than most people. Therefore any psychic ability, such as ESP, clairvoyance, telepathy, precognition, psychokinesis, etc., is a gift which very few individuals have.

Although palmistry and astrology are both communicable knowledge, I believe that genuine palmists and astrologers also have the natural gift of intuition. I am intuitive but not a psychic. Although I have studied palmistry and astrology, I prefer not to do readings out of fear of being inaccurate and misleading a person. Moreover, my spiritual teacher who taught me astrology and palmistry in India told me to do my readings free of charge, not even accepting a dime. I have strictly followed his instructions throughout my life.

Krista told me that she can also read horoscopes and was very proficient in astrology. I asked her to do a chart for Alice, to see if we were compatible. Alice was surprised to see that I, a scientist, actually have some faith in astrology and palmistry. She wondered how I managed to get a degree in science from Stanford. I told her she should talk to Krista, because she was an excellent astrologer and had gone out of her way to help me during my surgery.

As we were driving to Krista's house, Alice asked me, "If our charts don't match, are you going to dump me?" I assured her that I do not make life decisions based on astrological readings alone. For example, according to my astrological chart I will be luckier if I live close to an ocean or a big reservoir of water. But living near Lake Michigan did not help me to survive at the University of Chicago, and being by the Pacific Ocean did not help me to get straight "A" grades at Stanford. Moreover, I took the position at the University of New Mexico knowing that the nearest ocean is approximately 800 miles away. But I got my heart fixed and enjoyed my job.

Fortunately Alice's reading with Krista went well, and afterward she was not as skeptical about astrology.

A NEW LIFE OPENS UP

After my surgery Marilyn assured me that the darkness around my aura had disappeared, and that I would meet my future wife soon. As mentioned, Alice and I met shortly thereafter, in 1996. However, Marilyn also predicted that I would move to a different medical school. She herself then left for Chicago with her children to be closer to her family in Indianapolis.

In 1998 an opening came up at the University of Texas-Houston Medical School, and Professor Hunter offered me a job as a Full Professor. Professor Hunter was a tenured faculty at the University of Chicago, where he went to Emory University, and finally came to the University of Texas as a chair of the department. I was an associate professor at the University of New Mexico, and it was very tempting to move to a medical school at Texas Medical Center, the largest medical complex in the U.S.

In thinking about a possible move to Texas, I also had to consider Alice. If I decided to go, would she want to go with me? Were we truly compatible, and would our relationship even last? Alice was born in Santa Fe, went to school at the University of New Mexico, and was an only child like me. Still I had my doubts about us. Krista, however, assured me, based on our charts and her interaction with Alice, that we would move to Houston.

COMING TO HOUSTON

I accepted the position at the University of Texas-Houston Medical School and moved to the "Magnolia City." Alice remained behind temporarily and we managed to carry on a long distance relationship for a little over a year. Eventually on June 26, 1999, we got married and a year later, thanks to the outstanding support of Professor Hunter, my tenure was granted.

My parents started spending their summer months in the U.S. with Alice and me, until father started having health problems and could not travel anymore. Alice loves India and always visits it at least once a year, sometimes even twice a year. My spiritual teacher in India told me that Alice was born in India in a past life.

We moved Alice's parents from Santa Fe in 2010 due to their deteriorating health condition. My mother was critically ill in June 2011, and she was destined to die, as all medical options were exhausted. However, Alice's prayers miraculously saved her life (more on this in Chapter 4).

After a month my father passed away on July 31, 2011, and one day later Alice had a vision of seeing him in a white shirt as she drove out from our home. My father loved Alice as his own daughter. I myself had no such vision.

Our present life (2015) is full of worries because my mother is in such poor health. We cannot even bring her to the U.S. because of her condition. Both of my in-laws are also experiencing bad health. However, my mother's recovery from near death was a miracle, one that motivated me to write this book.

I have gone to several psychic fairs and at one of them I met Maria, a very gifted psychic. She had an intensely vivid OBE or out-of-body experience when she was a child and also as an adult. Alice, although she is not very interested in astrology, thinks there might be something to astrological readings and often asks me about our future.

PARANORMAL PHENOMENON (PARAPSYCHOLOGY)

Paranormal phenomenon, also known as parapsychology, extrasensory perception (ESP), or simply the sixth sense, includes telepathy, clairvoyance, precognition, presentiment (intuitive feelings about the future), psychokinesis (the ability of the mind to influence matter—for example, bending a spoon without touching it), out-of-body experience, psychic healing, after-death communication, remembering past lives, and others. The Society of Psychical Research was founded in London in 1882 to investigate paranormal phenomena from a scientific point of view, and since then many studies have been published regarding parapsychology.

In 1930 Dr. Joseph B. Rhine and his colleagues extensively researched various aspects of ESP at Duke University. Although based on many studies, Professor Rhine concluded that ESP is a real phenomenon. But many scientists had issues with his statistical analyses, and criticized his studies as being methodologically biased.

In the 1970s, due to an affiliation between the Parapsychology Association and the American Association for Advancement of Science (which publishes the noted journal *Science*), more investigators initiated research on parapsychology. Papers published in mainstream scientific journals, however, are full of conflicting reports, some in favor of psychic phenomenon and others finding no psychic abilities in individuals who claim to have them. In this chapter I cite a number of convincing reports showing evidence of ESP. In Chapter 5 I will discuss scientific research in the field of the near-death experience.

In the first decade of the 20th Century, a horse name Hans drew worldwide attention in Berlin as a famous thinking animal. Hans solved calculations by tapping numbers or letters with his hoof in order to answer questions. In-depth investigation, however, showed that the horse was able to give the correct answer by reading tiny "micro signals" in the face of the questioning person. As a result, in many ESP experiments face to face contact between persons is now avoided.[31]

MODERN PARAPSYCHOLOGY RESEARCH

The term "psi phenomenon" is often used in parapsychological research. It denotes an anomalous process of information or energy transfer that cannot be explained in terms of known physical or

---

31. Samhita L, Gross HJ. "The clever Hans phenomenon revisited." Commun Interf Biol 2013; 6(6): e27122.

biological mechanisms. Therefore, as expected, various forms of psi, such as precognition, psychokinesis, and telepathy, violate the well-established laws of physics.

In one study to evaluate the precognition capacity of 100 volunteers (50 male and 50 female undergraduates from Cornell University), pictures of two curtains appeared on a computer screen side by side. One screen had a picture behind it (of erotic images) and the other had no picture. The object was to click on the curtain to see the picture and each subject had 36 chances. The authors observed that participants correctly identified the future position of the erotic pictures more frequently, a 53.1% hit rate, compared to the 50% hit rate expected from chance alone. More interestingly, extroverts scored better than introverts, though there was no gender difference in the correct response rate.

However, in another experiment dealing with precognitive avoidance of negative stimuli, no positive result was observed. The authors further commented that if the psi phenomenon exists, it is not unreasonable to suppose that it might have evolved by conferring survival and reproductive advantages to our species. Therefore, psi phenomenon may be an evolutionary gift to humans, but few individuals are significantly gifted among the general population.[32]

It has been well documented that the left side of the brain is involved with language and logic, and that the right side of the brain is involved with creativity and intuition.[33] Some investigators report involvement of the right brain in psychic phenomena. However, Moulton and Kosslyn, using a neuroimaging technique, found no difference in subjects when exposed to psi stimuli and non-psi stimuli, and concluded that there is no existence of the psi phenomenon.[34]

In contrast, Bonilla commented that the materialist paradigm, which considers the brain as the sole cause of consciousness and psychic phenomena, has been challenged by a new model that seems to demonstrate that psi may have an extra brain origin. The author

---

32. Bem D. "Feeling the future: experimental evidence for anomalous retroactive influences on cognition and affect." J Pers Soc Psychol 2011; 100: 407-425.
33. Corballis MC. "Left brain, right brain: facts and fantasies." PloS Biol 2014; 12: e1001767.
34. Moulton ST, Kosslyn SM. "Using neuroimaging to resolve the psi debate." J Cogn Neurosci 2008; 20: 182-192.

hypothesized that psychic phenomena are associated with a cosmic field or cosmic consciousness.[35]

Several studies have shown that the human body can apparently detect randomly delivered stimuli (sound versus silence, or emotional versus neutral images) one to ten seconds earlier than actually receiving such stimuli. This phenomenon, which is called "predictive anticipatory activity," resembles precognition and is also considered psi activity.

In a study conducted by McCraty et al, 30 calm and 15 emotionally arousing pictures were shown to 26 participants. The authors observed that the heart appeared to receive information before the brain, and there were significant differences in ECG (electrocardiogram) and EEG (electroencephalogram; recording of brain waves) prior to visualization of emotionally arousing versus calm pictures. The authors also observed that the frontal cortex, temporal lobe, occipital lobe, and parietal lobe areas appeared to be involved in the processing of pre-stimulus information (intuitive information before seeing an image).[36]

The findings of this scientific paper are fascinating because in the tantric tradition, the heart chakra is involved in processing stimuli, most notably emotional stimuli. The heart chakra may be blocked due to a failed relation, death of a loved one, or emotional distress.

Many scientific experiments have been conducted on telepathy. Results are often conflicting. Laboratory experiments, however, indicate that mental intention can weakly influence another subject sitting at a distance. Further studies show a suggestive correlation between EEG results in isolated pairs, including the student-teacher relationship. Overall, research in this field indicates that roughly 15% of isolated pairs of people show a non-chance, positive EEG correlation.

Radin et al conducted a study using thirteen pairs of volunteers (eleven pairs of adult friends and two mother-daughter pairs), where one volunteer relaxed in a steel-walled, electromagnetically and acoustically shielded room, while the other volunteer (of the pair) was located in a

---

35. Bonilla E. "Is the brain the creator of psychic phenomenon or is a paradigm shift inevitable?" Invest Clin 20`13; 55: 103-106 [article in Spanish].
36. McCraty R, Atkinson M, Bradley RT. "Electrophysiological evidence of intuition: Part 2-A system wide process." J Altern Complement Med 2004; 10: 325-336.

dimly lit room 20 meters (approximately 66 feet) away. The second person was stimulated at random times by the live video images of the first person. The authors observed that three out of 13 pairs of volunteers (23% of the subject pairs) showed a significant correlation between the brain waves (EEG) of the sensorially isolated subject and the other subject sitting at a distance and randomly seeing images of the sensorially isolated person.

Amitava's father, center, with his brother and sister, 2008.

Although the mechanism of such phenomena is currently unknown, the authors speculated that it might be related to a "quantum entanglement" in which two isolated physical systems display correlated behavior as if they are not physically separated. For example, two electrons separated from each other may show similar behavior, as if they are still together.

Quantum entanglement is presently understood as an exceedingly fragile state, quite unlike the stable, hot, and wet environment of the human brain. Yet, a general understanding of the mathematic model, using higher dimensions, theoretically indicates that such phenomena may occur even in a stable condition, such as conditions in the human brain.[37] Physics already mathematically demonstrate the existence of dimensions beyond the four dimensions (the three classical dimensions, plus time, the fourth dimension), but the existence of higher dimensions has not yet been validated by experiments.

Various studies conducted in the last 70 years support the reality of telepathy. Conscious intentions may have the capacity to affect another living system at a distance, which is the basis of the positive effects of intercessory prayers and healing energy in the case of distance healing. However, only specially gifted people have such capabilities, and several studies used them as subjects in their experiments. Imaging studies indicate that paranormal phenomena like telepathy is associated with activities of the right hemisphere of the brain.

In one study the authors used Mr. Gerard Senehi, a 46 year old with well-known psychic abilities, such as mind reading, telepathy, and telekinesis. The control subject was a 43 year old man with no paranormal ability. The investigators drew an image, but neither the psychic nor the control subject had any access to the picture. Functional Magnetic Imaging study (fMRI) was performed on both subjects when they psychically attempted to view the image drawn by an investigator. The subject with the paranormal gift, Mr. Senehi, drew an image that was strikingly similar to the original picture. The picture drawn by the control subject (with no psychic ability), however, was not at all similar to the original image.

Interestingly, analysis of the fMRI image of the psychic showed significant activation of the right brain (*parahippocampal gyrus*) while no such activation was found in the control subject. However, during telepathic exercise his left brain (center for reasoning) was activated (left inferior frontal *gyrus*). Therefore, the limbic system of the brain may be involved in telepathy.[38]

Another study attempted to understand the neurobiological basis of the psychic ability of Mr. Sean Haribance, who has routinely experienced "flashes of the image" of objects hidden from him, and is also

---

37. Radin D. "Event related electroencephalographic correlation between isolated human subjects." J Altern Complement Med 2004; 10: 315-323.
38. Vankatasurbramanian G, Joyakumar PN, Nagendra HR, Nagaraja D et al. "Investigating paranormal phenomenon: functional brain imaging of telepathy." Int J Yoga 2008; 1: 66-71.

capable of providing accurate personal information about people with whom he is not familiar. The specificity of details for target pictures correlated with alpha activity lie in his brain in the occipital lobe (responsible for visual activity). Further studies using single photon emission computed tomography (an advanced brain imaging technique) showed increased activity within the parietal lobe and occipital region of his right brain during paranormal activity. The authors concluded that the right hemisphere of the brain (right parietotemporal cortices or its thalamic inputs and hippocampal formation) is responsible for paranormal activity.[39]

In another study the authors investigated the mechanism behind the psi abilities of artist Ingo Swann, who helped develop the process of remote viewing (awareness of distant objects or places without employing normal senses).

The authors asked him to sit in a quiet chamber and sketch and verbally describe distant stimuli (pictures or places). The proportions of the unusual 7-Hz spike in his brain waves and the slow wave activity over his occipital lobe per trial moderately correlated with accuracy between these distal hidden stimuli and his responses. The MRI study also indicated a different structural and functional organization within the parieto-occipital region of the subject's right hemisphere (right brain) during paranormal activities.[40]

Some people can see color around a human being, which is referred to as an "aura." In New Age language the aura is a subtle energy field that surrounds a person or object. Traditionally the human aura has seven colors that match the seven chakras (or "wheels"), the energy centers of human body. A trained aura expert can visualize the aura as a halo color field surrounding the body, while different layers of the human aura are tinted with colors that determine the character of a person and their physical condition, as well as their present state of mind. Some experts think auras can be photographed using special

---

39. Roll WG, Persinger MA Webster DL, Tiller SG et al. "Neurobehavioral and neurometabolic (SPECT) correlates of paranormal information: involvement of the right hemisphere and its sensitivity to weak complex magnetic field." Int J Neurosci 2002; 112: 197-224.
40. Persinger MA, Roll WG, Tiller SG, Koren SA et al. "Remote viewing the artist Ingo Swann: neuropsychological profile, electroencephalographic correlates magnetic resonance imaging and possible mechanism." Percept Mot Skill 2002; 94: 927-949.

techniques, such as Kirlian photography. Seeing auras may not require a spiritual gift since a person can be trained by an aura expert to see them.

There is a neurological condition called "synesthesia" in which stimulation of one sensory or cognitive pathway leads to automatic, involuntary experiences in a second sensory or cognitive pathway. Synesthesia is due to cross-wiring in the brain, as individuals with synesthesia have more synaptic connections than normal people across brain regions. Since the brain regions responsible for the processing of each type of sensory stimuli are intensely interconnected, people with synesthesia may associate people, voices, letters, numbers, objects, even musical tones, with particular colors. It has been estimated that one in every 2000 people (synesthetes) has synesthesia, and more than 60 different types of synesthesia have been described.

A person may be born with synesthesia or may acquire it as a result of head trauma or various other causes, for example, practicing meditation. Milan et al commented that visualizing auras around a person may be related to synesthesia. The authors observed discrepancies, however, between aura readings provided by four volunteers with synesthesia and two expert aura readers who do not have synesthesia.[41] In general, people with synesthesia are gifted with artistic talents. It has been speculated that the famous actress Marilyn Monroe may have had synesthesia.

SHOULD WE MAKE IMPORTANT LIFE DECISIONS BASED SOLELY ON ASTROLOGICAL OR PSYCHIC READINGS?

Before answering this question let me tell you about a report published in the *New York Times* on the front page, June 6, 2015.[42] A 32 year old man from Brooklyn spent $713,975 on a psychic named Priscilla Kelly Delmaro, over 20 months in his long quest to be reunited with the woman he loved.

In the summer of 2013 the man was melancholy despite having a good job, because he had met Michelle and was in love, but the woman

---

41. Milan EG, Iborra O, Hochel M, Rodriguez-Artacho MA et al. "Auras in mysticism and synesthesia: a comparison." Conscious Cogn 2012; 21: 258-268.
42. *New York Times*, June 6, 2015, page A1, continued on page A16.

was not in love. On August 24 he found a psychic in New York, Delmaro, who told him that he and Michelle were "twin flames," but negativity was keeping them apart. The man paid Ms. Delmaro $2500 on the first visit and $9,000 on the second visit. He later gave her a diamond ring worth $40,064 so that she could protect herself, and she later advised him to visit Michelle, who was then living in Los Angeles. The trip, however, proved fruitless.

She then told him that a spirit was following him. In order to get rid of the spirit, the man continued spending money.

In December, Ms. Delmaro informed him that she had to lure the spirit over a gold bridge in the other realm so that it could be trapped. He gave Ms. Delmaro another $80,000 to build an 80 mile bridge on the Other Side. On February 17, 2014, he found out from a Facebook page that Michelle had died nine days earlier, possibly from a drug overdose. At that point Ms. Delmaro told him that she could place Michelle's spirit into the body of a 31 year old woman.

One year and many more payouts later, Ms. Delmaro bled the man of everything he had. The man started borrowing money from friends and colleagues, and finally the psychic told him to go to Los Angeles to find Michelle. He met a woman in California who Ms. Delmaro later said was the "new" Michelle. However, the woman was 24, not 31 and Michelle did not seem to be inside her.

At this point the man returned to New York and sought out the help of Mr. Nygaard, a private investigator, and together they went to the police in May 2015. Bank statements were given to the detectives: the man had paid a total of $713,975 to the psychic. Ms. Delmaro and her companion were arrested on May 26, 2015, in a restaurant in Midtown Manhattan and were charged with grand larceny. They remained in jail during the publication of the *New York Times* report. Their lawyers denied the man's allegations.

When I was in Chicago and had a failed relationship, I went to a psychic who told me that an evil spirit was following me, and unless it could be trapped by a gifted psychic, all my future relationships would fail and I would be single for the rest of my life. The price of getting rid of the evil spirit was $10,000, but after that, if I could provide her with a picture of a single woman I wished to marry, for another $10,000 we would get married, and live happily for ever after, just like a fairy tale.

I agreed and went to a music store close by and bought a record of Madonna (she was single at the time) with her picture printed on the jacket. I thought investing $20,000 was a wise decision, if I could marry Madonna and spend the rest of my life with her. When I went back to the psychic she was furious and threw me out. She even forgot to charge me $10, her initial consultation fee.

On another occasion, this time in India, my friend referred me to a gifted astrologer who, after reading my astrological chart, recommended that I wear a ring containing a very expensive gemstone (approximately $50,000) on my left index finger. He assured me that I would receive the Nobel Prize within 10 years. I agreed, but on one condition: he must sign a legal document prepared by a lawyer stating that if I get the Nobel Prize within the next 10 years, I would share 50% of the prize money (approximately $500,000) with him; but if not, I would return the ring and he would pay me $100,000 ($50,000 of my investment money plus another $50,000 for pain and suffering due to the false promise). He kicked me out of his chamber.

As a scientist I believe in psi phenomena and psychic ability. However, a truly gifted psychic is very hard to find. Extrasensory mental abilities require extraordinary mental control, as well as extreme concentration. As a result, many gifted individuals are hesitant to use their powers to earn a living. Some individuals even prefer to be loners and live in their own spiritual world. Therefore, the most difficult part is to a find a truly gifted psychic; one who can predict future events accurately, so that all of one's important life decisions can be made based on psychic predictions alone.

Although my wife's astrological chart matches my chart, I would have married her even if they were incompatible, because her actions show how much she loves me. When we got married she left behind a stable job, a good life with many friends, and her parents in New Mexico, to be with me in Houston. Therefore, in general my recommendation is to use your own judgement and advice from friends and family, as well as your gut feelings, to make important decisions. If you trust a psychic and you have seen that his/her predictions came true in the past, you can certainly take their psychic input into account.

Let me give you another example.

I went to school in California, and in general I love the state. My astro-cartography chart also indicates that a very favorable Jupiter line passes through California, and as a result, the area between Los Angeles and San Francisco Bay is the luckiest place in the world for me to live. In 2009 I had a job offer from a good hospital in California, but during my interview I picked up some red flags. Therefore, despite California being an auspicious place to live, based on my gut feeling during the interview, I decided not to accept the offer. Not all jobs in California will make me happier than my current job. However, if Stanford University offers me a job, I will accept it in a heartbeat.

As I mentioned earlier, it is very difficult to find a truly gifted psychic. I have met few "psychics" who are truly psychic, and only Bistu Babu (see Chapter 2) showed an accuracy rate close to 100% in his readings: as he predicted, I came to the U.S. in 1980, did research and clinical service, taught resident physicians in a medical school, married a professional woman with red hair, and we bore no children.

Going to a psychic fair is usually hit or miss. As noted, most "psychics" have no psychic gifts. I have never had a reading from a celebrity psychic who charges between $500-1000. Therefore, I cannot comment on the accuracy of their readings.

Once, after attending Stanford University, I went back to India for a visit and asked Bistu Babu why he had no desire to use his gift to become a multimillionaire. He smiled and replied that psychic gifts are not for making money. God grants this particular gift for serving people. He also said that if I had a thorough knowledge of the Other Side, I would never need to ask him a single question. Unfortunately, Bistu Babu "kicked the frame" (the guru's term for "passed away") in 1984, and I have yet to meet another psychic of his caliber.

Always be aware of fake psychics. Here are some tips:

- A truly gifted psychic never fishes for information, but always starts off with a reading that closely resembles one's life. If more than 60 percent of his/her statements are accurate, then the psychic must have real gifts, because something is unlikely to be true by chance alone.
- After the reading a gifted psychic never asks for more money. If you are satisfied by his/her reading, you give something extra out of appreciation.

- A truly gifted psychic never claims that he/she can change your luck or solve your problems. The reading is guidance, but a good psychic recommends that you use your judgement and gut feelings when making important life decisions. Moreover, a good psychic will never claim that he/she is always right.
- If a psychic asks you for more money than the reading fee, for example, for buying expensive candles or to remove a curse (the amount of money may be few hundred dollars to thousands of dollars), please run. I never encounter these types of "psychics" at psychic fairs or in metaphysical bookstores. Professional psychics charge between $20 and $100 for a 30 to 60 minute reading. I have met at least two fraud psychics that I know of. I was attracted to a psychic store with a bright neon sign and a consultation fee of $5 in one case and $10 in another. However, after the reading one woman wanted $500 for removing a negative spell, and the other wanted around $10,000. In both cases I ran away as fast as I could. I am not saying that if a psychic charges $5 to $10 she/he must be a fraud. Another time I talked to a gifted psychic in Albuquerque who only asked for a donation, but she was very accurate about my past (and some future events that happened later). However, she did not ask for anything more than a donation. I gave her $50 and she told me that was too much. She would only accept $40 for a 50 minute reading. She told me she uses her God given gifts to help people.
- Usually it is cheapest to go to a psychic fair for a reading, and if you think the psychic is not accurate you might waste around $20-$25. As mentioned, reasonable psychics, depending on geographic location, may charge between $30 and $100. In an expensive place, for example, New York City, a psychic may charge more. My personal upper limit is $100 for a 30 minute reading.
- If a psychic tells you that you have a curse, or a demon is chasing you, and in order to remove such a curse hundreds if not thousands of dollars will be needed, leave. There is no such thing as a personal or family curse. If a psychic scares you, please consult a religious or spiritual person, such as a Christian pastor, a

Jewish rabbi, or a Hindu priest. A holy person can counsel you, and if necessary remove the evil force free of change, or for a small donation. If you have a personal relationship with Jesus, ask for his help. His divine power can remove any evil at no cost to you.

CONCLUSIONS

According to the Vedas we humans come from a universe of eternal joy. Throughout our lives here on the planet earth we float on an ocean of joy, then at death we go back to the universe of eternal joy, our original home. Life is short and therefore it is important to live in harmony with others.

Bistu Babu told me that *happiness comes from inside one's self, not from the outside, and that all of us are beings of light having a human experience.* He also told me that a gifted psychic never has a set fee. He or she accepts donations, or a small fee, which anyone can afford. He also told me that true psychics live simple spiritual lives.

Although psychics are born not made, sometimes psychic gifts run in a family. Moreover, several of my spiritual teachers told me that all humans have psychic gifts, but most people do not care to develop their psychic abilities. Through meditation, prayer, and living a religious and or spiritual life, one may gain or improve his or her psychic powers.

4

FROM HINDU SKEPTIC TO CHRISTIAN BELIEVER

A LATE NIGHT PHONE CALL

I vividly remember the night of June 16, 2011, when my phone rang around 2 AM. I thought my resident was calling me regarding a laboratory test result concerning a drug overdosed patient. But it was my cousin Tukun, calling from Kolkata, India. He informed me that he had taken my mother to a local hospital due to a high fever convulsions, and that she had been admitted by Dr. Nag. I also know Dr. Subimal Choudhury, a very well respected physician, and the former dean of a prestigious medical school in India. I called Dr. Choudhury and begged him to help my mother, and gave him the contact information for Dr. Nag. Dr. Choudhury told me not to panic, and promised he would contact Dr. Nag. I gave him my telephone number at work.

I spent a sleepless night, but went to work the next day anyway. Around 11 AM, June 17, the phone rang. It was Dr. Choudhury. He told me to take the next available flight to Kolkata. Despite all efforts by the medical team, mother was not responding to any therapy and was having multi-organ failure. Her convulsions could not even be controlled by medication. The medical team had no choice but to put her on ventilation so that I could say goodbye to her.

I immediately walked into my boss' office, telling him the situation. He granted me an emergency family medical leave. I called United Airlines and there was only one business class seat left to fly to Frankfurt using Star Alliances' partner Lufthansa, with a connecting flight to Kolkata. Fortunately, the United Airlines agent was able to issue me the ticket. It was expensive, but I did not care. My wife drove me to the Bush Intercontinental Airport to catch a 4:30 PM flight. I had roughly $200 cash with me, as I did not have time to go to the bank.

THE MOST DIFFICULT FLIGHT OF MY LIFE

I boarded the plane and it took off on schedule. I was not in the mood to eat a business class dinner, but I ate it anyway. A few minutes later I went to the bathroom and threw up. A flight attendant noticed my peril and politely asked me if I was okay. I shared with her that my mother was dying. She felt sorry for me and promised to pray for her.

We landed at Frankfurt and I immediately called my aunt in Kolkata. She told me that mom was in critical condition and that everyone was

Jesus giving the Sermon on the Mount, whose core teaching is the all-important eight Beatitudes. Jesus patterned these eight blessings on Buddha's "Noble Eight-Fold Path," which he learned while studying in India under various Buddhist and Hindu masters during his 18 "lost years" (from ages 12 to 30).

praying for her. She suggested that I also pray. I boarded the flight to Kolkata. When lunch was served I politely told the flight attendant that I was not hungry. She assured me that high quality Indian food was available.

I told her my situation and also informed her that I was not able to keep my dinner in my stomach during my flight from Houston to Frankfurt. She advised me to try hot soup and a little bit of lamb curry with rice. I was hungry so I ate. Fortunately I did not throw up this time. Later she upgraded me to first class so that I could lie down and rest. I was deeply touched by her kindness.

I tried to get some rest, but even a comfortable first class seat did not help. The flight landed at Kolkata on June 18 at around 11 PM local time, and my heart was beating faster wondering if mother was still alive.

I rushed through immigration and customs and was relieved to see Ganesh waiting at the airport for me. Ganesh owns a car service and lives in my neighborhood. Probably my aunt arranged for him to meet me. He informed me that my mother was still alive, but that I should go to the hospital immediately and visit her in the ICU. I had only a carry-on bag and we rushed to the car.

SEEING MOTHER AT HER DEATHBED

Ganesh drove as fast as possible and within 20 minutes we arrived at the hospital. I ran through the corridor and went to the ICU. Mother was under artificial life support and the night resident physician offered his sympathy for her condition. I asked him if I could examine her and he agreed.

Mother had no reflex and she was in a deep coma with occasional convulsions. The resident physician explained to me that they had tried everything, but failed to resolve her condition. I looked at the monitors. Everything looked hopeless. As a last resort I reviewed her laboratory reports, which indicated that she had multiple organ failure. I cried and regretted not bringing my wife along. I thought I was so strong that I had discouraged her from accompanying me.

Ganesh was waiting outside and I decided to let him go. I wanted to spend the night at my mother's bedside, but it was not allowed. Ganesh drove me to our apartment and my aunt was with my father, who was suffering from Alzheimer's disease. Mother had been his sole caregiver.

My aunt comforted me and suggested that my wife Alice should come as soon as possible to say goodbye to mother.

Another sleepless night passed. I called Dr. Choudhury in the morning and he too confirmed that nothing could be done medically, and that eventually I must decide when to withdraw her life support.

Around 8 AM, June 19, I went back to the hospital and talked to the head of the medical board. But other than sympathy he had nothing else to offer. I asked him if life support could be continued for few more days so that my wife might say goodbye to her, and he agreed.

I returned home and called my wife and asked her to come as quickly as she could. It was nighttime in Houston. She called me back fifteen minutes later saying she was flying the next morning, taking the 10:40 AM United flight to Tokyo, to connect with a Thai flight to Bangkok. From there, after a two-hour layover, she would take another Thai flight, this one to Kolkata. She told me her arrival time: 11:50 PM local time on June 21. She cried on the phone and told me to hope for a miracle.

Later I took a cab to go to Dakshineswar Kali temple (founded by Rani Rashmoni, a wealthy women from Kolkata, around 1854) where Saint Ramakrishna (1836-1886), the guru of swami Vivekananda, was able to see Goddess Kali and have a conversation with her. I had visited the temple many times with mother, because she insisted I should go with her. This was the first time I went on my own. I sent up my silent prayer and asked forgiveness for all of the bad behavior I had engaged in during my life.

MY WIFE ARRIVED AT KOLKATA

My physician friend Krishnajyoti, who was also involved with my mother's care, did not allow me to go to the airport alone. The flight landed on time and Alice, with tearful eyes, was the first passenger to come out of the custom enclosure. She had a carry-on bag and we headed for the car immediately.

We arrived at the hospital and rushed into the ICU. My wife had a prayer book and she started praying. Krishnajyoti and I were looking at the monitors, thanking God that mother was still alive. Alice cried out loud and the nurse in charge of night shift told us we could stay as long as we wished.

Suddenly the night resident physician came to me very excited and said, "look at the monitors now!"

POWER OF PRAYER

Krishnajyoti and I could not believe our eyes. Signs of life were coming back. The resident physician tested mom and her pain reflex had returned. My wife was unaware of these events, as she was still praying for mother, telling God, "let thy wish be fulfilled."

Suddenly mother opened her eyes for the first time in six days. It was 2 AM and a miracle was happening right before me. Alice quickly realized that there was still hope and continued praying. Meanwhile, the resident physician, Krishnajyoti, and myself stood there spellbound, wondering how mother's survival could be explained from existing medical knowledge.

We all decided not to discontinue her life support next morning. This is because she was now seizure free, and medications, which had not done anything for the last five days, now started working. I decided not to wake up Dr. Choudhury or Dr. Nag at that late hour.

Krishnajoyti dropped us home around 3:30 AM and my aunt hugged Alice. I told her about the miracle and my aunt commented that Jesus answered Alice's prayer. I slept some that night, but the scientist inside me told me not to get too excited just yet.

MOM'S RECOVERY: A TOTALLY UNSCIENTIFIC EVENT

The next morning, around 7 AM, I called mother's attending physician Dr. Nag at his residence. He had graciously given me his home number.

He first thought that I was hallucinating, because he had examined my mother the previous night around 11 PM, and signed the document indicating that life support could be suspended the next morning, as her chance of survival was next to nothing. I begged him to call the hospital to check mother's status. He called me back and said that she was opening her eyes and that the night staff considered Alice a saint because she had performed a miracle. I corrected Dr. Nag, saying that it was Jesus, not my wife, who performed the miracle. But my wife certainly prayed to Jesus to help mother.

Dr. Nag thanked me and said that he was going to the hospital to check mom, and asked me to come. I also called Dr. Choudhury and he said he had witnessed only one such miracle in his 45 years of medical practice. He told me to meet him at the hospital, and also to bring my wife.

Alice and I were at the hospital by 8 AM, and soon after Dr. Nag arrived. He literally ran to the ICU. Fifteen minutes later he came back saying that he had never witnessed anything like it in his life. He greeted my wife as if she were Mother Teresa. We discussed what to do next and we both agreed to repeat the blood tests to check her kidney and liver function.

Dr. Choudhury arrived around 9 AM, and after examining

mother, he had the same opinion: *she had come back from death.*

We decided to wait for the laboratory test results, which arrived around 10:30 AM. They indicated that her kidneys and liver were functioning normally again.

Alice and I went back to the Dakshineswar Kali temple and later to St. James Cathedral, an old Christian church in Kolkata, and prayed for mother's full recovery. Around 6 PM we went back to the hospital and were pleased to hear from the nurse that her condition had improved dramatically throughout the day.

Dr. Nag and Dr. Choudhury decided to extubate (remove life support) from mom the next morning, June 23, and insisted that Alice pray during the procedure. I was afraid my wife might faint since the operation was not pleasant to watch, and if mother could not breathe on her own, there was a chance that she could die instantly.

Next morning mother was extubated. She was able to breath normally all by herself. We stayed at the hospital for another hour and everything was fine. Alice was present in the room during extubation, and did not pass out. Mother was transferred from the ICU to a private room. Dr. Choudhury had to leave, but Dr. Nag and my wife and I celebrated by going to a restaurant for some good Indian food.

MY MOM CLEARLY SAW TWO ANGELS WITH ALICE AT HER BEDSIDE BUT DID NOT SEE ME

More surprises awaited me.

The next day, June 24, when Alice and I visited mother, she asked Alice where her friends were staying. I told her that Alice had come alone. But mother did not believe me, and repeatedly asserted that she saw two very beautiful women wearing white robes accompanying Alice. I told her that only Krishnajyoti and I were at her bedside, while Alice was praying. But she did not see Krishnajyoti or me. "When can I go back to the house and see your dad?" she asked. I assured her that she would be discharged from the hospital soon.

That night Alice and I had a long discussion. My aunt immediately declared that the "two beautiful women" were angels sent by God to take care of mother. I did not say anything, but my entire worldview, based on the teachings of my atheist father, was shaken to its core. Mother was so confident about her vision that I could not call it a hallucination. Moreover, she had not been taking any hallucinogenic drugs. Maybe Karl Marx was wrong. Religion is not "the opiate of the masses." Maybe there actually was something bigger than science and medicine.

Mother was out of danger and Dr. Nag told me that he would discharge her from the hospital within a week. She had been admitted to a private hospital and we now needed to pay her medical bill. I had only $200 and my wife had around $100. My cousin kindly took care of the cost, and I paid him back later.

Alice and I flew back to the U.S. on June 28, but mother was still in the hospital. So Tukun took care of her by arranging home health care nursing. Before leaving Kolkata, Alice kissed my dad and he opened his eyes with full clarity. Then he spoke a few words to me after almost two years of silence: "Take care of yourself and Alice." I had witnessed another medically improbable event.

Tukun drove us to the airport and assured us that he would take care of everything. Mother fully recovered and was able to take care of dad who had Alzheimers. Sadly, dad passed away on July 31, a month after mom's full recovery. Alice and I promptly returned to India.

DR. CHOUDHURY ALSO WITNESSED A MIRACLE

I shared my mom's vision with Dr. Choudhury, and he said that he had only witnessed one other such incident in his entire career.

A Buddhist monk, who was also the head of a monastery, was critically ill and there was no hope for his survival. When Dr. Choudhury informed his fellow monks that life support should be discontinued, they asked to pray for him one more time. One monk told Dr. Choudhury that the head of the monastery did not select his successor, and maybe he could come back from death in order to complete this important task. Dr. Chaudhry laughed, but silently. He did not want to insult these deeply religious men.

He stayed in the room when the monks started circling the dying monk, chanting something in a foreign language. After ten minutes of prayer, the dying monk opened his eyes. Dr. Choudhury could not believe it.

To make a long story short, the monk completely recovered and said that Lord Buddha had granted his prayer, allowing him to come back from death. He also told his followers that he had only two weeks to live to complete his task. He was discharged from the hospital a week later, went back to the monastery, and one week after selecting his successor he passed away. Dr. Choudhury admitted that it was a miracle.

SOME MEDICAL MIRACLES RELATED TO CHRISTIANITY

Although I had gone through some transformation after my mother's miraculous recovery, skepticism was not totally purged out of my system.

According to the Myers-Briggs classification system, the famous English nurse Florence Nightingale had an introverted-intuitive-thinking-judging personality. This might explain why she claimed to have received a call from God when she was only 16 years old; one commanding her to serve humanity for the rest of her life.[43] However, my mother is an extrovert and has no intuition, although she is a religious person. Therefore, her vision during her coma cannot be explained by her personality type.

The scientific method originated with three English intellectuals: Francis Bacon, John Locke, and Isaac Newton. It was under their influence that in the late 18th Century physicians at the University of Edinburgh reaffirmed that medicine is strictly a secular profession. Scientific explanations are materialistic and thus, according to science, God will always remain an enigma. From the scientific perspective, the cosmos is unemotional, mechanistic, directionless, and uncaring as it endlessly repeats cause and effect, strictly following natural laws. In short, science holds that all natural phenomena can be explained by these laws, leaving no room for the divine, the soul, or miracles.

In contrast, religion maintains that nature is a creation of a loving God and that miracles are his gifts; gifts to be hoped for, but not expected, by the faithful believer. A miracle then is an act of God, and proof of spirit as well as the active presence of the divine.[44]

I started my own research to see if there is anything in the mainstream medical literature regarding the scientific explanation of

---

43. Dossey BM. "Florence Nightingale: her personality type." J Holist Nurs 2010; 28 (1): 57-67.
44. Jones JW, McCullough LB. "Medicine versus religion in the surgical intensive care unit: who is in charge?" J Vasc Surg 2013; 57: 1146-1147.

medical miracles.

Miracles are well reported throughout written history. Jesus Christ was the greatest miracle healer known to mankind, and many people witnessed such miracles, all which were documented in the Bible. Duffin, a reputed physician, examined more than six hundred miracle records in the canonization files of the Vatican's Secret Archives from the 17th Century to 20th Century. Commenting on them from a medical standpoint, he asserted that some of these miracles could not be explained by current scientific knowledge.[45]

From February 11 to July 16, 1858, Marie Bernarde Soubirous, an uneducated 14 year old girl born into a poor family in Lourdes, France, had eighteen visions of the Virgin Mary at the Massabielle Grotto. Later, she took vows and became a nun, passing away in 1879. Her canonization came in 1933. Thirteen cases of water cures at the grotto were reported in 1858, and the local bishop regarded seven of them as miracles. Since then millions of people have travelled there in hope of receiving their own miraculous cure.

In 2008, at the 150th anniversary of the vision of the Virgin Mary, approximately nine million people visited Lourdes. Sixty-seven cures that occurred there have been acknowledged by the Roman Catholic Church as miracles. Moreover, in 1954 an International

The savior Vishnu, one of the three gods of the pre-Christian Hindu Trinity, Trimurti.

---

45. Duffin J. "The doctor was surprised: or how to diagnose a miracle." Bull Hist Med 2007; 81 (4): 699-729.

Medical Committee, comprised of 20 university professors of medicine and skilled specialists, reviewed numerous documents and certified that 26 events were miraculous cures.

Francois et al thoroughly examined 25 of the Lourdes cures acknowledged as miracles between 1947 and 1976, as well as an additional 411 patients who were also cured. Writing from a medical point of view, they concluded that the Lourdes phenomenon is extraordinary in many respects, and cannot yet be explained by science. Thus the miracles at Lourdes concern both science and religion.[46]

MEDICAL MIRACLES REPORTED IN RECENT MEDICAL JOURNALS

Medical miracles are also reported in the mainstream medical literature in which the recovery of numerous patients lies beyond current scientific understanding. Joyce Martin, NP, RN, a family nurse practitioner, reported a medical miracle performed by God on New Year's Day.

As she was getting ready to go home after a long day's work at the hospital, a child who had been accidently shot by his brother with a 22-caliber rifle, was brought in. The nurse tried to place an endotracheal tube (a tube placed through the throat to initiate artificial life support), but his vocal cords were not visible due to the blood in his airways. His pulse was 30, indicating he was collapsing and would die without immediate life support.

The nurse prayed according to her Christian beliefs, after which, surprisingly, a tube could be placed easily during the fourth attempt. Moreover, the patient's pulse and blood pressure normalized. The trauma surgeon operated on the boy, and after stablizing he was transferred to a regional hospital. However, the odds of his survival were poor. And even if he managed to live, he would certainly be impaired—or so it was believed.

Over the next few days the child took a turn for the worse, but Ms. Martin continued to pray. Two days later, when she went to see him, the excited staff reported that he was improving and that he had

---

46. Francois B, Sternberg EM, Fee E. "The Lourdes medical cures revisited." J Hist Med Allied Sci 2014; 69(1): 135-162.

perked up between 11 and 12 on Sunday during church hours.

Nine days after the accident the boy recovered enough to ask for a hamburger. He had had three near death experiences. During the last one, he was told by his grandfather to go back because "it was not his time." The medical team believed the boy's survival was a miracle performed by God. Most surprisingly he recovered completely without any impairment.[47]

Nath et al published a scientific paper entitled, "Miracles Still Happen: A Rare Case of a Self-inflicted Penetrating Injury of Ear." In it the authors describe the case of a patient who had a sharp carpenter's nail transverse the entire thickness of his skull, with the pointed end coming out at the opposite temporal area of the brain. Removing the nail posed a great danger, as it had already violently impacted the inside of the skull bone. Certainly if he survived the patient would be hearing-impaired with substantial brain damage. And yet, miraculously he made a full recovery after surgery. No hearing loss. No brain damage. Such an event cannot be explained by the known principles of medical science.[48]

Dr. Susan Gold of Pennsylvania State University Hershey Medical Center recently reported in the prestigious *Journal of American Medical Association* (JAMA) the miraculous survival of a patient named James, who had heart failure due to infarction (heart attack). He also suffered from kidney and liver failure, along with sepsis. The patient was placed on an ECMO (Extracorporeal Membrane Oxygenation) machine, which is a medical device to treat a critically ill patient where both the heart and lungs are not functioning. The author concluded that the survival of James was a miracle.[49]

There are numerous other reports of miracles in the medical literature (searching PubMed.com alone I discovered 70 articles on this topic that have been published in peer-reviewed medical journals). Discussing all of them, with proper citation, would make this chapter unnecessarily long. But the take home message is that a number of critically ill patients with less than 1 percent chance of survival have

---

47. Martin JB. "Miracle on New Year." J Christ Nurs 2010; 27(2): 112-113.
48. Nath B. Sarkar P, Das T. "Miracles still happen: a rare case of self-inflicted penetrating injury of ear." Indian J Otolaryngol Head Neck Surg 2011; 66(1): 107-109.
49. Gold SA. "A piece of mind." Miracle. JAMA 2014; 311(15): 1499.

virtually come back from death and gotten well. And yet their miraculous recoveries cannot be explained by any branch of science.

CONCLUSIONS

"There are more things in heaven and earth, Horatio, than are dreamt of in your philosophy." This immortal line from *Hamlet* is very applicable to the many accounts of medical miracles that go beyond science. Although medical miracles do not happen every day, if you talk to experienced physicians who treat critically ill patients, you will be surprised to hear at least one or two stories of miraculous recoveries that have no scientific explanation.

Today, we enjoy many benefits from modern science, but at the same time science has its limitations. A counter argument would be that no one living in the 19th Century could imagine a day when Man would step foot on the moon. Maybe at some point in the future science will be able to demystify medical miracles. However, until then let us accept the restrictions of science and have faith in God.

5

A GLIMPSE OF HEAVEN: NEAR DEATH EXPERIENCES

INTRODUCTION

Although I have never had a near death experience (NDE), in May 1994, during my open heart surgery at the University of New Mexico Hospital, I had a pleasant OBE. I felt myself floating above my physical form as it lay on the operating table, where surgeons were busy patching the hole in my heart. I moved freely through the walls of the operating room, glided down the corridor, and floated outside the hospital to look at the Sandia Mountains. Suddenly I felt a strong pull back to my body, and everything was blank thereafter. Some might call this a partial NDE.

When my senses came back that evening in the surgical ICU, I hated my body due to the severe pain and discomfort, and for the next few days I wished I had never come back to the physical plane. However, no one believed my story because I was familiar with the setting of the operating room, as well as the surgeons, nurses and resident physicians involved in my surgery. Moreover, certain anesthetics such as ketamine (sometime used in children for anesthesia) can produce an out-of-body experience, as there are reports of near death experiences from ketamine abuse. Later I checked my medical records and found that ketamine had not been used during my surgery.

During my recovery I discussed the incident with my friend Krista. She was the only one who believed me because as a child she had several surgeries with accompanying OBEs similar to mine. She could easily pass through walls, and on one occasion she saw her parents sitting in a room worrying about her operation. Krista had never visited or seen that room before. When she accurately described her experience to her parents, they confirmed that they had been sitting in that specific room and were anxious about the outcome of her procedure.

Our psychic friend Maria also had out-of-body experiences when she was a child, as well as a vivid one when she was 42, where she had a glimpse of the Other Side. During her heavenly visit she met her deceased father and her deceased grandmother. Her grandmother told her that it was not her time, and Maria felt a strong pull to go back to her body. She repeatedly tells us, especially during very hot and humid summer days in Houston, that the temperature on the Other Side is "just perfect." Maria had her last NDE-like experience at home when she did not feel well and, tellingly, was not facing any life-threatening illness.

SCIENTIFIC RESEARCH ON NEAR DEATH EXPERIENCES

What happens when people die has intrigued human beings throughout time. Death can be defined as the loss of all vital signs, including cessation of heart beat, respiration, and brain functions (death by cardiorespiratory criteria). While cardiac arrest is the final step that defines death irrespective of cause (except brain death, where respiratory and circulatory function can be maintained artificially), with advances in resuscitation science, death by cardiac arrest may be reversed in some patients.

Recollections reported by many patients throughout the world where death was reversed (they were pronounced dead at some point) by advanced medical techniques, are considered near death experiences.[50] In general NDEs are defined as intense psychospiritual experiences, characterized by an atypical state of consciousness which occurs during life-threatening conditions. However, NDEs have also been reported in individuals (like Maria) who were not facing life threatening situations. Near death experiences may occur in a healthy individual during meditation, depression, isolation, and during critical life events. Moreover, a healthy individual who is present at the time of a close relative or friend's death may have an NDE.[51]

---

50. Parnia A. "Death and consciousness-an overview of the mental and cognitive experience of death." Ann N Y Acad Sci 2014; 1330: 75-93.
51. Moody RA, Perry P. *Glimpses of Eternity.* Amazon digital edition, 2013.

The first comprehensive modern report about the near death experience was published by Raymond Moody, M.D., Ph.D., in his international bestselling book *Life After Life* in 1975.[52] This book is based on 150 cases of NDEs in which Dr. Moody identified 15 characteristics of near death experiences described by survivors. These close encounters with death provide compelling evidence for the Afterlife. However, many scientists have attempted to explain away the phenomenon of the near death experience using a biological or physiological hypothesis.

In his book Dr. Moody defines an NDE as "any conscious perceptual experience occurring in individuals pronounced clinically dead or who came close to death." Common features include an overwhelming sense of joy and peace, complete absence of pain, an OBE, passing through a tunnel and then coming out into a bright light, communication with dead relatives, a life review, and finally travelling back into the physical body (Table 1). One of the reasons it is believed that near death experiences are a glimpse of heaven is the positive transformation of the individuals who have them. Most become more spiritual or religious, and no longer fear death.

Amitava's wife, Alice Moore in 1999, Paris, France.

In his 1989 book *Life Beyond*, Dr. Moody extensively studied nearly 1000 cases of near death experience, providing more evidence that NDEs are real and not hallucinations. Moreover, many patients

---

52. Moody RA. *Life after Life*, Bantam Press, 1975.

reported that they had never felt such overwhelming joy and peace before in their entire lives.[53]

There are many other books on the topic of the near death experience. Some are personal accounts, including the one of reputed physician Dr. Eben, published in 2012.[54] After reading these works, many people, including both myself and my coauthor, are convinced that there is an Afterlife. However, there are still atheistic skeptics who consider the near death experience nothing more than a brain-generated program purposefully designed by evolution; one meant to ease one's final moments before slipping permanently into nihilistic oblivion.

PREVALENCES AND CHARACTERISTICS OF NEAR DEATH EXPERIENCES

NDEs are occurring with increasing frequency because of improved survival rates due to modern techniques of resuscitation. Taking data from scientific publications and public polls, it appears that roughly 15 to 20% of critically ill patients and some 5% of the general population have had near death experiences.[55] This means that approximately 13 million Americans have had near NDEs in recent years.

Other studies report that 15.5% patients who survived cardiac arrest (in a population of 116 patients) had a near death experience. In a British study of 63 survivors of cardiac arrest, 11% had NDEs. An analysis of nine studies in four countries yielded an average estimate of 17% critically ill patients having near death experiences.[56] Interestingly, the frequency of NDEs is higher in young people than older people. Ring reported that 48% of people with near death experiences had a mean average age of 37 years.[57] Morse observed that 85% of the

---

53. Moody RA. *The Life Beyond*. Bantam Press, 1989.
54. Alexander E. *Proof of Heaven: A Neurosurgeon's Journey into the Afterlife*. Simon and Schuster, 2012.
55. Dacco E, Agrillo C. "Near death experiences between science and prejudice." Front Human Neurosci 2012; 6: 209.
56. Khanna S, Greyson B. "Near death experience and spiritual wellbeing." J Relig Health 2014; 53: 1605-1615.
57. Ring K. *Life at Death: A Scientific Investigation of the Near Death Experience*. Coward McCann and Geoghenan, 1980.

children he studied had had near death experiences.[58]

Most studies involving NDEs have been conducted in patients with life-threatening cardiac arrest or in patients with severe traumatic brain injury. However, few studies have been done on individuals having near death-like experiences during non-threatening situations, such as epilepsy, syncope (fainting or passing out characterized by a fast onset, short duration, and spontaneous recovery, most likely due to low blood pressure), intense grief, anxiety, etc. Greyson et al reported that out of 100 patients who had seizures, seven (7%) had an out-of-body experience.[59]

In another study the investigators compared the NDEs of 50 patients with pathological coma with the near death-like experiences of 140 patients who did not have life-threatening conditions. Interestingly, it was found that real near death experiences after coma were similar to near death-like experiences occurring in patients during non-life threatening events. The most frequently reported feeling (in both groups) was peacefulness (89-93%). Overall 188 patients had positive near death experiences, while only 2 patients reported negative experiences.[60] Greyson also studied 272 psychiatric outpatients who had significant psychological distress, including a close encounter with death. Sixty one patients (22%) reported having an NDE.[61]

NDEs have been found in all age groups and there are many accounts of children having them. Interestingly, there are reports of near death experiences in children as young as 3 years of age. This is revealing because children this age have not yet developed concepts about death or the Afterlife.

In his book *What Happens When We Die*, Dr. Parinia described the case of Andrew, who at the age of three and half years had an NDE during open heart surgery. Approximately two weeks later he asked when he could go back to that beautiful sunny place with all the flowers

---

58. Morse M. *Parting Visions: A New Scientific Paradigm in the Near Death Experience: A Reader.* (Bailey LW, Taytes J, editors). Routledge, New York and London, 1996, pages 299-318.
59. Greyson B, Fountain NB, Derr LL, Broshek DK. "Out of body experiences associated with seizures." Front Human Neurosci 2014; 8: 65.
60. Charland-Verville V, Jourdan JP, Thonnard M, Ledoux D et al. "Near-death experiences in non-life threatening events and coma of different etiology." Front Hum Neurosci 2014; 8: 203.
61. Greyson B. "Near death experiences in a psychiatric outpatient clinical population." Psychiatr Serv 2003; 54: 1649-1651.

and animals. His father said he could take him to a park, but Andrew said that it was not a park, but a very lovely area where he met a lady who loved him and floated with him.

A year later, while watching *Children's Hospital* (a television program filmed in a hospital), Andrew saw a child undergo heart surgery. He got excited and said that his doctors had used the same machine (a bypass machine) on him—which is startling, because Andrew was under anesthesia at the time. His dad reminded him that he was asleep during the operation. Andrew replied that this was true, but that nonetheless he had seen his body lying on the operating table: he and a lady were floating near the ceiling looking down at it. Later, when shown a photograph, Andrew identified the "lady" as his deceased grandmother.[62]

Morse et al reported the NDEs of four children, which included a sense of being out-of-body, travelling through a tunnel or up a staircase, seeing beings dressed in white, and a decision to return to earth. The authors concluded that the near death experiences of children are similar to those of adults.[63] Interestingly, near death experiences have been reported across all cultures and among all religious groups. Even atheists have them. While the central experience is universal in nature, interpretation of the experience appears to be influenced by personal, religious, or cultural views.

GREYSON NDE SCALE

Although there are various ways to determine if someone has had a near death experience, a scientific measuring stick developed by Greyson, known as the Greyson NDE scale (published in 1983), is widely used by researchers to scientifically establish it in a subject. The initial scale contained 33 questions based on the experiences of knowledgeable subjects describing their 74 near death experiences. The author included 16 questions in the scale, and a score for each question which varies from 0 to 2, based on the response. A total score of 7 and above in the scale indicates a near death experience. This reliable, valid

---

62. Parnia S. *What Happens When We Die?* Hay House, 2005.
63. Morse M, Conner D, Tyler D. "Near-death experiences in a pediatric population: a preliminary report." Am J Dis Child 1985; 139: 595-600.

and easily administered yardstick is clinically useful in differentiating near death experiences from organic brain syndromes and non-specific stress response.[64] The questions included in the Greyson NDE scale are listed in Table 2 at the end of this chapter.

NEAR DEATH EXPERIENCES AND POSITIVE LIFE TRANSFORMATIONS

Near death experiences are profoundly mystical, spiritual, or religious in nature, and have long term positive transformational effects. Many people who have had an NDE often report less or no fear of death and a greater sense of altruism, the latter which is evidenced by greater empathy and selflessness, less materiality, and increased faith and spirituality. In Table 3 commonly encountered positive transformations after near death experiences are listed.

In one published report, the author studied 37 patients for six months who had out-of-hospital cardiac arrest. Of the 37 patients, seven (18.9%) had near death experiences. The author observed that patients who had an NDE are more tolerant of others, have greater concern about social justice, a higher sense of the inner meaning of life, and a greater appreciation of nature, compared to patients who had no NDE. The authors concluded that in general cardiac arrest survivors do not express extensive life changes, except for survivors who had near death experiences. Therefore, the near death experience can transform a person's life in a very real and positive way.[65]

Dialysis patients are susceptible to life-threatening conditions, such as uremic coma before dialysis, as well as during dialysis, low blood pressure (hypotension), increased risk of sepsis, and cardiovascular events. Lai et al studied 710 dialysis patients at 7 centers in Taipei, Taiwan, and out of these patients 45 (or 6.3%) had near death experiences. Some patients experienced more than one NDE, bringing the total number to 51. The patients who had near death experiences were reported to be kinder to others and more motivated than those

---

64. Greyson B. "The near death experience scale. Construction, reliability and validity." J Nerv Ment Dis 1983; 171: 369-375.
65. Klemenc-Ketis Z. "Life changes in patients after out-of-hospital cardiac arrest: the effect of near death experiences." Int J Behav Med 2013; 20: 7-12.

who did not.[66]

Van Lommel et al in a large study of 344 cardiac patients who were resuscitated after cardiac arrest, observed that 62 of them (18%) reported one or more aspects of the classic NDE. But of these 62 patients, 41 had something much closer to a full blown NDE. For example, before intubating one 44 year old comatose patient, his health care team removed his dentures from his mouth. A week later when he was stable, he identified the physician who did this, even though the patient was comatose at the time. He also correctly described what was happening to him in the emergency room, for he was observing it all while floating above his body. The authors describe the most common features of NDEs in most of the patients studied, as well as two of the least common: the life review (8 patients) and the presence of a border in heaven (2 patients).

By the time of a two year follow up, 19 of the original 62 patients had died. But the authors were able to interview 37 patients, and after eight years, 23 patients. Patients who had near death experiences were more empathic and many showed increased intuitive feelings. Most people in the group showed more tolerance towards others and a strong belief in the Afterlife, as well as almost no fear of death. Positive changes were more significant after eight years than after two years.

In contrast, cardiac arrest survivors who did not have near death experiences showed less positive transformations in life, and most people in that group had both a fear of death and little belief in an afterlife.[67]

In general, the depth of spiritual well being in individuals who had NDEs correlates with the depth of such experiences. However, one negative aspect of near death experiences is that some individuals may find it difficult to readjust to earthly life, and may also be more emotionally vulnerable. Some people who have near death experiences are reluctant to share their experience for fear of being ridiculed by friends and family. However, with more research and evidence in the

---

66. Lai CF, Kao TW, Wu MS, Chiang SS et al. "Impact of near death experiences on dialysis patients: a multicenter collaborative study." Am J Kidney Dis 2007; 50: 124-132.
67. Van Lommel P, van Wees R, Meyers V, Elfferich I. "Near death experience in survivor of cardiac arrest: a prospective study." *Lancet* 2001; 358: 2039-2045.

future, society will inevitably become more accepting of the reality of NDEs.

SOME CASE REPORTS OF NEAR DEATH EXPERIENCES
Most reported near death experiences include profound feelings of peace, joy, and cosmic unity. Less familiar are the reports of disturbing near death experiences, which are full of darkness or nothingness, or are simply hellish. Greyson and Bush classified these unpleasant NDEs under three categories.[68]

1. The most common type has all the features of pleasurable near death experiences, such as an out-of-body experience, rapid passage through a tunnel towards a bright light, etc. But such positive experiences may be misinterpreted by an individual as distressing because he or she has no control over the events.
2. Less commonly occurring NDEs involve a sense of non-existence or eternal void.
3. The third and rarest type of negative NDE includes graphic hellish imagery, such as hideous landscapes, annoying noises, the presence of people in pain and distress, frightening animals, and demonic figures.

I will now discuss cases of both pleasurable and hellish NDEs. Based on numerous reports, the estimated incidences of distressing near death experiences range from 1% to 15%, indicating that negative uncomfortable experiences are far less common that positive blissful ones.

Case 1: Cooper described an interesting case where an African man in his mid-twenties had an NDE that occurred while being tortured (to elicit information). He was repeatedly escorted from his cell to a torture chamber, where he was kicked, punched, and beaten with batons and whips. During one especially violent session he felt himself rising towards the ceiling of the torture chamber and looking down at his body being abused below. He felt that he had left all his sufferings behind, and

---

68. Greyson B, Bush NE. "Distressing near death experiences." *Psychiatry*, 1992; 55: 95-110.

also observed a bright white light, as well as a sound like ocean waves. During the NDE images flashed before him; for example, visions of himself as a baby, as well as future visions, like the birth of his as of yet unborn first child. In between these flashes he continued to see his physical body lying on the floor below being tortured. The bright light then formed a tunnel, and he saw his physical body below starting to fade away as his "real self" began to move up the tube. The experience ended in his losing consciousness. Using the Greyson criteria for assessing near death experiences, the author concluded that this person's experience was a true positive NDE.[69]

Case 2: A seven year old girl nearly drowned in community swimming pool, but fortunately a physician was present at the scene who found her comatose. She then received CPR (cardiopulmonary resuscitation) and was also intubated (a medical procedure where a tube is inserted through the mouth for artificial respiration). She was immediately transferred to a local hospital, and then to a specialized children's hospital where she required mechanical ventilation. She regained consciousness on the third day of her hospital stay and was discharged a few days later. Two weeks after her near drowning episode she returned to school.

She was interviewed to see if she could recall the experience. She said that she only remembered talking to the heavenly father, but did not want to go into further detail. On her second interview she provided more information about her experience of drowning and dying. She had seen a dark tunnel and was scared, but a woman named Elizabeth appeared and the tunnel became bright. The woman was tall and together they walked into heaven.

She was excited to tell her interviewer that heaven was a fun place, bright and full of flowers. She also noticed a point-of-no-return border around heaven, but could not see past it. Additionally, she met her dead grandparents, her maternal aunt, and Heather and Melissa—two adults waiting to be born. She then met the heavenly father and Jesus, who asked her whether she would like to return to earth. The girl replied no, but when she was asked a second time

---

69. Cooper M. "Near death experience and out of body phenomenon during torture." Torture 2011; 3: 178-181.

whether she would like to see her mother again, she said yes, and woke up in the hospital.[70]

Case 3: A 15 year old boy was in a state of awareness during an elective surgery under general anesthesia. He remembered hearing music (which the surgeon confirmed), the voices of the doctors, someone who had moved him onto his left side during surgery (this was also confirmed), and an injection in his hip. But none of the classic aspects of an NDE.

However, three years earlier, at the age of 12, he had experienced a genuine NDE during another uneventful surgery. He felt as though he had suddenly woken up from sleep, then had an OBE in which he saw his physical body lying below on the table surrounded by doctors. He was floating up near the ceiling of the room at the time. He then felt a sensation of detachment from his physical body, and a feeling of lightness.

Next he saw a dark tunnel, which he passed rapidly up and through. At the end of the tunnel there was a bright light that he could look at without hurting his eyes. During this he also heard noises, which later turned into voices. Suddenly he was once again attached to his physical body, marking the end of the NDE.[71]

Case 4: A man from southeastern Brazil went to prison at age 19 for four homicides and drug trafficking. After 3 years in prison he was attacked by other prisoners for revenge, and was stabbed 14 times. Later the prisoner reported a spiritual experience during surgery where he saw himself descending into the depths of hell, and then a divine hand removed him and raised him into the air.

He was eventually lifted into a cloud from where he observed brights lights and a golden city (possibly the "Holy City" or "new Jerusalem" featured in the book of Revelation).[72] He wanted to go to that golden city, but a voice told him that he was not ready, for he still had a mission on earth to accomplish. Then the hand brought him back to his body, and he was surprised to be alive.

---

70. Morse M. "A near death experience in a 7-year old child." Am J Dis Child 1983; 137: 959-961.
71. Lopez U, Forster A, Annoni JM, Habre W et al. "Near death experience in a boy undergoing uneventful elective surgery under general anesthesia." Paediatr Anaesth 2006; 16: 85-88.
72. See Revelations 21:1-27; 22:1-5.

After the incident he changed, regretting his crimes. Still a prisoner, he started to get involved with religious activities, even offering to stay in the same cell with his former enemy (a man who tried to kill him several times). In 2011, after 26 years in prison, he was granted a conditional release. He now lives in metropolitan São Paulo, where he works as a salesperson. During his interview he said that (based on his NDE) his faith prevents him from returning to crime.[73]

Case 5: Howard Storm, a successful tenured art professor at Northern Kentucky University, found that he had a perforation in his small intestine (duodenum perforation, a very painful medical condition) during a trip to France. He needed emergency surgery. However, it was a Saturday and the hospital had a difficult time finding a surgeon. He was afraid he was going to die and gave an impassioned farewell to his wife who was at his bedside.

The elephant deity Lord Ganesha, son of Shiva and Parvati, is one of the five primary divinities of Hinduism. The god of wisdom, wealth, and education, Ganesha's worship crosses all Hindu divisions and sects, making him one of the most popular of Asia's deities.

Storm almost lost consciousness, then found himself standing by his bed, but feeling no pain. He tried to communicate with his wife and another man in the room, but they could not hear him.

Suddenly he heard people calling his name in English, without any French accent. He left the room and started walking with them

---

73. Braghetta CC, Santana GP, Cordeiro O, Riggnatti SP et al. "Impact of a near death experience and religious conversion of a criminal: case report and literature review." Trends Psychiatry Psychother 2013; 35: 81-84.

down a long hallway. When he asked questions he was told to shut up. When he refused to walk any further, his guides pushed him; when he fought back, they tortured him. His body now ripped apart, he collapsed on the ground. At that moment he heard a voice inside his head advising him to pray to God. However, being an atheist he had forgotten how. He then remembered a prayer he had learned as a child:

> The Lord is my shepherd; I shall not want. He maketh me to lie down in green pastures: he leadeth me beside the still waters. He restoreth my soul: he leadeth me in the paths of righteousness for his name's sake. Yea, though I walk through the valley of the shadow of death, I will fear no evil: for thou art with me; thy rod and thy staff they comfort me. Thou preparest a table before me in the presence of mine enemies: thou anointest my head with oil; my cup runneth over. Surely goodness and mercy shall follow me all the days of my life: and I will dwell in the house of the Lord for ever.

As he was praying the figures told him that "there is no God," and that if he continued they would hurt him. Despite the threat Storm went on praying and the demonic forms eventually backed off.

He then asked Jesus to rescue him from the hellish place. Immediately he felt Jesus' hand reaching out to him, then lifting him up. As this was occurring he experienced a profound love coming from Jesus. He realized that his life had deteriorated after adolescence when he had become a selfish unloving person, and began engaging in heavy drinking and adultery. Jesus told him to go back to earth.

After surgery he woke up from anesthesia and spoke to his wife. "It's all love and you don't have to suffer anymore," he told her. Being an atheist, however, she did not like his story of the angels and Jesus, and their marriage ended.

He grew desperate to learn more about the Bible as well as for fellowship in a church. It was then that he began to attend Christ Church in Fort Thomas, Kentucky. Feeling a call to minister, he attended the United Theological Seminary in Dayton, Ohio, and became a pastor. He described his experience in his book *My Descent Into Death*.[74]

SCIENTIFIC HYPOTHESES ATTEMPTING TO EXPLAIN NEAR DEATH EXPERIENCES

There are many scientific hypotheses which seek to explain the phenomena associated with NDEs using our current knowledge of psychology and neurobiology. However, there are many questions unanswered by these theories and, as a result, some scientists are convinced that near death experiences cannot be explained scientifically. Let us look at the major hypotheses regarding NDEs, focusing on their strengths and weaknesses.

ANOXIA OF THE BRAIN

Anoxia of the brain means oxygen is no longer reaching the brain due to an interruption of the blood supply. Without a supply of oxygen brain cells (neurons) usually start dying within a minute and after 10 minutes recovery of the patient becomes extremely difficult. Anoxia of the brain affecting the cerebral cortex, hippocampus, and the limbic system may be associated with feelings of floating and an out-of-body sensation.

However, when anoxia is induced slowly, such as by high altitude, alcohol, or a drug overdose, features of NDEs are usually absent, indicating that the rapid onset of anoxia is needed for near death experiences. Fighter pilots ascending to high altitude rapidly sometimes experience anoxia and may report pleasurable feelings, such as pleasant emotions or out-of-body experiences, but never full blown near death experiences.

Only a few children suffering from reflex anoxic seizures (a non-life threatening condition where anoxia may result due to holding the breath) reported features of near death experiences. But most children did not remember anything at all during the event.[75] Another major limitation of this hypothesis is that it cannot explain the NDEs of individuals who have no life-threatening condition.

---

74. Howard Storm. *My Descent Into Death*. Harmony, 2005.
75. Blackmore S. "Experiences of anoxia: Do reflex anoxic seizure resemble near death experiences?" J Near Death Studies 1998; 17: 111-120.

TEMPORAL LOBE HYPOTHESIS

The temporal lobe of the right brain (right hemisphere) is often referred to as the "God spot" by neuroscientists because it is activated during religious or spiritual experiences. Stimulation of the temporal lobe is known to induce hallucination, memory flashbacks, and OBEs. Acute stress and hypoxia (inadequate oxygen supply) during a life threatening event may render neurons in the temporal lobe hypersensitive, thus reducing seizure threshold.

Sometimes patients suffering from temporal lobe epilepsy report profound spiritual experiences similar to NDEs. Moreover, near death experiences also alter sleep patterns, for example, causing shorter duration of sleep and delayed REM (rapid eye movement) sleep—which may be related to altered temporal lobe functions.

Based on a study of 43 patients, Britton and West concluded that individuals who have near death experiences may be physiologically distinct from other populations with respect to altered temporal lobe functions.[76] However, NDEs can occur in a perfectly healthy person. Thus the temporal lobe hypothesis fails to adequately explain them.

DRUG INDUCED OUT OF BODY EXPERIENCE

Many drugs are administered during the resuscitation process, including anesthetics, and so some investigators claim that near death experiences are nothing more than drug induced phenomena. It is true that an anesthetic such as ketamine may cause an out-of-body experience when abused by adults. In one study of 50 drug abusers (out of 125 interviewed by the authors) who had near death experiences (Greyson's NDE score of 7 or higher), most abusers (45 drug abusers) reported having them when they started misusing drugs, such as ketamine, cannabis, and ecstasy.

The most common features of these types of experiences included an altered perception of time (90%), a strong sense of detaching from the physical body (88%), and a sense of peace or joy.[77] Ketamine abuse alone can induce these experiences, especially OBEs, because

---

76. Britton WB, Bootzin RR. "Near death experiences and temporal lobe." Psychol Sci 2004; 15: 254-258.
77. Corazza O, Schifano F. "Near death states reported in a sample of 50 misusers." Subst Use Misuse 2010; 45: 916-924.

ketamine is a dissociative anesthetic agent. However, in real life the majority of people who have NDEs are not drug abusers. Moreover, ketamine is rarely used in treating critically ill patients. Conclusion: the drug-induced hypothesis does not explain near death experiences.

Endogenous endorphins (morphine-like compounds produced by the human brain) or the neurotransmitter serotonin can sometimes be responsible for near death-like experiences. Serotonin is closely associated with mood. Endorphins are natural opioid-like compounds which are often secreted by the brain under stress. The "runners high" phenomenon experienced by many long distance runners, including marathoners, is due to the secretion of endorphins by the brain. Endorphins can be produced by the brain during physical trauma, including fear of impending death.

The secretion of endorphins results in pain relief, feelings of well being, and intense pleasure, all which may suggest that endorphin release causes positive emotions during near death experiences.[78] Although, reported less commonly, negative emotions may occur in patients due to hellish near death experiences. Thus, the endorphin hypothesis fails to fully explain the NDE.

Serotonin, which is associated with a positive mood (deficiency may cause depression), has also been suggested as a trigger molecule for near death experiences.[79] But again, it is difficult to explain distressing NDEs using the serotonin hypothesis.

CENTRIPETAL ISCHEMIA OF THE RETINA

A reduced or lack of blood supply to the retina, known as centripetal ischemia of the retina, has been proposed as a mechanism causing tunnel vision during NDEs. Sometimes fighter jet pilots flying at high altitude experience this phenomenon. Visual cortex inhibition due to lack of blood supply (anoxia) has also been postulated as an explanation for tunnel-like perception.[80]

However, during sudden acute brain damage secondary to

---

78. Carr D. "Endorphins at the approach of death." *Lancet*, 1981, February 14: 390.
79. Morse ML, Venecia D, Milstein J. "Near death experiences: A neurophysiological explanatory model." J Near Death Studies 1989; 8: 45-53.
80. Blackmore S, Troscianko T. "The physiology of tunnel vision." J Near Death Studies 1988; 8: 15-28.

cardiac arrest, it is very unlikely that one would have a tunnel vision due to retinal dysfunction, because the brain is much more sensitive to anoxia than the eyes. Also, fainting does not cause tunnel vision; although the blood supply in the retina may be reduced.

Furthermore, many of the descriptions given by NDEers who have travelled inside a tunnel on the Other Side are extremely detailed. Such descriptions include, for instance, noticing various sparkling colors in the tunnel's walls, watching the tunnel revolve slowly as they speed through it (usually on their backs, moving feetfirst), seeing other "souls" travelling with them or passing them from the other direction, hearing unearthly beautiful music, and smelling various lovely aromas. The very fortunate traverse the entire tunnel, coming out into a bright light and a realm of pure love and wonderment, where they often encounter deceased loved ones, friends, and even pets.

The centripetal ischemia of the retina theory cannot begin to explain any of these particular features, let alone many others, of the near death experience. Conclusion: fail.

OTHER NEUROBIOLOGICAL MECHANISMS

The neurobiological theory of near death experiences implies that in order to have one, a person must have a brain disorder. For example, patients with temporal lobe epilepsy often report out-of-body experiences, possibly due to hyper-activation of the amygdala and the hippocampus. Moreover, brain lesions, brain damage, and the pharmacological side effects of therapy (anesthetics, opioids, steroids, etc.) may yield a picture of delirium which commonly occurs in patients in intensive care units. But the features of delirium are entirely different from near death experiences.

Nelson proposed that REM intrusion (a condition that occurs when some characteristics of the common REM sleep state—for example, rapid eye movement, low muscle tone, and dreaming—are activated during wakefulness) may be responsible for near death experiences, because the resuscitation process may induce this state in individuals who are prone to REM intrusion. Based on a study using 55 subjects who had near death experiences, the authors observed that sleep paralysis, as well as sleep related visual and auditory hallucinations, were substantially more common in subjects who had near death experiences compared to the control population.[81] However, the hypothesis of REM intrusion is not compatible with cardiac arrest where brain activity is silent.

PSYCHOLOGICAL INTERPRETATIONS

According to the expectation hypothesis, NDEs are a product of an altered mental state due to life threatening conditions. This is because stressful conditions can trigger something akin to a near death experience due to the projection of one's religious or cultural beliefs (for example, a belief in an afterlife). This is the reason Christians may meet Jesus, Jews may meet Abraham, and Buddhists may meet Buddha during NDEs.

According to the birth hypothesis, going through a tunnel and seeing a bright light at the end is exactly what one would expect to experience during an NDE, because the brain is merely playing back its recording of the memory of one's own birth experience. In another hypothesis, depersonalization or personality disorder may predispose such experiences. However, the duration of cardiac arrest, the degree of anoxia, the duration of unconsciousness, and the administration of medicines were reported to be irrelevant, and could not predict the occurrence of an NDE.

In addition, psychological factors also did not contribute to the occurrence of near death experiences, because fear of death, prior knowledge of NDEs, and religious beliefs were again found to be irrelevant. Therefore, while these scientific hypotheses may be somewhat relevant to understanding near death experiences scientifically, given their persistent lack of proof and vague and insufficient explanations, they remain nothing more than theories.[82]

DO NEAR DEATH EXPERIENCES VALIDATE AFTERLIFE?

In many ways near death experiences are universal, and for most people such experiences are profoundly transcendental, mystical, and spiritual or religious in nature. Many individuals describe being in a

---

81. Nelson KR, Mattingly M, Lee SA, Schmitt FA. "Does the arousal system contribute to near death experience?" *Neurology*, 2006; 66: 1003-1009.
82. Facco E, Argillo C. "Near death experiences between science and prejudice." Front Hum Neurosci 2012; 6: 209.

As the date of Jesus' birth was not recorded by early Christians or historians, it was borrowed from Paganism, most of whose savior-gods were—like the Hindu Chrishna, the Egyptian Horus, the Greek Dionysus, and the Persian Mithra—born on December 25.

beautiful place during their NDE, one whose description defies human language. A few people have also reported negative near death experiences, which were full of darkness, horror, and the presence of demonic entities. Nearly all religions in the world profess the presence of heaven and hell. Therefore for many, near death experiences support the concept of an afterlife.

Although many scientists attempt to explain near death experiences from a physiological and neurological point of view, there are still many unanswered questions. For example, published reports clearly validate one important aspect of NDEs: a profound positive transformation in the person who experiences one. However, non-NDE patients who faced similar life threatening events do not report any major change in their lives. Common sense tells us that both groups of patients should experience a positive transformation, because both came close to death and faced their own mortality.

Then why is it that only patients who have had NDEs show positive modifications in their lives, as well as overcoming the fear of death? Common sense again tells us that they must have witnessed something profound that convinced them that death is not the end and that there is an afterlife. As such, physical death here on earth must be a form of "birth" in the spirit world.

More convincing proof that NDEs are real and that they provide a glimpse of heaven is based on the facts that

• the NDEs described by children are similar to those depicted by adults (children are not culturally or religiously primed to believe in an

afterlife).
• the characteristics of near death experiences are similar worldwide.
• no single physiological, psychological, neurochemical, or neuroanatomic hypothesis can explain every aspect of NDEs.
• multifactorial models based on a combination of various criteria, such as brain hypoxia and the release of serotonin and endorphins by the brain, cannot explain all the features of near death experiences.[83]

In a paper published in the prestigious *Journal of the Royal Society of Medicine* (U.K.), Susan J. Blackmore, Department of Psychology, University of the West of England, questioned the validity of describing NDEs as drug-induced hallucinatory experiences. The author argued that near death experiences often happen to people who think they are dying when there is no serious medical emergency. In fact, an OBE may happen to a perfectly healthy person, thus eliminating the drug induced hallucination hypothesis.

It is true that the details of NDEs may vary; for example, Christians tend to see Jesus, while Hindus may see the messengers of Yamraj coming to take them away (they often refuse to go). Yet, the general pattern of near death experiences are very similar across cultures, indicating that religious expectations are not responsible for most of the characteristics of near NDEs.

From a religious standpoint, suicide attempters should have hellish experiences. But, in fact, their NDEs are sometimes similar to positive ones. Just as interesting, such experiences tend to reduce future suicide attempts.

In short, none of the proposed theories explain either *all* NDEs or *all* of the features of NDEs, and thus many investigators argue that something beyond the brain is involved; for example, that there is a soul, or something else, that leaves the body at death.

Conclusion? Near death experiences *are* actual glimpses of the Afterlife.[84]

In order to investigate whether they had positive NDEs or not, Ring and Franklin interviewed thirty-six persons who had been close to

---

83. Bonilla E. "Near death experience." Invest Clin 2011; 52: 69-99 [article in Spanish].
84. Blackmore S. "Near death experiences." J Royal Soc Med 1996; 89: 73-76.

death as a result of a suicide attempt. Seventeen, or 47 per cent of the subjects, described positive NDEs. Furthermore, these were more common among men than women. Interestingly, suicide-related NDEs did not differ from the NDEs reported in medical journals in patients suffering from cardiac arrest or other life-threatening illnesses.[85] It would seem that people who commit suicide due to terminal illness, mental illness, or confusion as a result of severe emotional distress, are forgiven by God and get a second chance to grow spiritually when they return to their bodies.

This begs the question: does an individual attempting suicide have a distressing NDE as spiritual punishment because he or she is trying to hurt others or to get revenge? Barbara Rommer M.D., observed that 55% of people who attempted suicide had negative near death experiences. She coined the word LTP (less than positive) NDEs, and observed that 19.4% of people who had LTP NDEs identified themselves as either atheist or agnostic prior to their near death experience. If a person disrespects life, he or she may be prone to LTP. She also divided LTP near death experiences into four categories:[86]

1. Positive near death experiences interpreted wrongly.
2. Near death experiences involving very unpleasant feelings of an eternal void.
3. Diabolical near death experiences with a vision of hell.
4. Near death experiences involving frightening life reviews.

However, with time people who had LTP NDEs considered them to be a blessing in disguise, because their lives were transformed in positive ways—similar to those who have positive NDEs. For example, during one frightening near death experience a woman fought with a demonic being, and for the first time in her life she called on God for help. Immediately she felt the genuine presence of the Almighty, as well as communication with him. This type of life changing event cannot be explained by any known scientific theory.

In their study Thonnard et al noted that memories of NDEs

---

85. Ring K, Franklin S. "Do suicide survivors report near death experiences?" *Omega*, 1981; 2: 191-208.
86. Rommer B. R. *Blessing in Disguise: Another Side of the Near Death Experience.* Llewellyn, 2000.

contain more self-referential and emotional information, as well as better clarity, than expected from memories of someone in a coma. The authors concluded that near death experiences should not be considered imagined event memories.[87]

Parina and Fenwick commented that since NDEs can occur when the mind (the collection of all our thoughts, feelings and emotions) and consciousness (self-awareness) appear to be functioning—despite a non-functional brain—then consciousness may be a separate scientific entity in its own right. It has been proposed that this concept falls under the auspices of quantum mechanics, and it may well. But currently there is no scientific proof.[88] Aspects of NDEs that appear to support the concept of an afterlife are listed in Table 5.

NEAR DEATH EXPERIENCES IN BLIND AND VERIDICAL NEAR DEATH EXPERIENCES

Blind case studies provide compelling proof that near death experiences are indeed paranormal phenomena that cannot be explained by science. Additionally, veridical NDEs, where out-of-body experiencers observe events or gather information that can verified by others upon their return to a conscious state, offer further evidence that such experiences are paranormal in nature.

Ring and Cooper published the results of an investigation of 31 blind people who had OBEs and other aspects of the near death experience. Their investigations revealed that blind individuals, including those blind from birth (ten subjects), had NDEs similar to sighted people. Some who are blind from birth have neither any concept of light or any visually based knowledge prior to their NDE, indicating that most likely near death experiences are a form of transcendental awareness. The authors provide details of some of their subject's experiences, which are very convincing that NDEs in the blind are indeed the same as sighted people. An example is Vicki Umipeg.[89]

---

87. Thonnard M, Charland-Verville V, Bredart S, Dehon H et al. "Characteristics of near death experiences memories as compared to real and imagined event memories." PLoS One 2013; 8: e57620.
88. Parinia S, Fenwick P. "Near death experiences in cardiac arrest: visions of a dying brain or vision of a new science of consciousness." *Resuscitation* 2002; 52: 5-11.
89. Ring K, Cooper MA. "Near-death and out of body experiences in the blind: A study of apparent eyeless vision." J Near Death Studies 1997; 16: 101-147.

Ms. Umipeg, a 43 year old married woman (at the time of the publication of the report), was born prematurely (22 weeks old at birth) and suffered from severe optic nerve damage that made her blind from birth. She had two NDEs, one when she was 12, and another, which was more vivid, at age 22 during a car accident. In the midst of the latter she had an out-of-body experience, then came back. She had yet another profound experience while being transferred from the accident scene to the Harborview Hospital in Seattle.

However, Vicki had no memory of her trip to the hospital, but after arriving she found herself up on the ceiling watching a male doctor and a woman working on her body. She also overheard their conversation, which had to do with possible damage to her eardrum that could cause deafness. She tried to tell them that she was fine, but they could not hear her and she received no response.

After that Vicki floated through and above the ceiling, where she had a brief panoramic view of the surrounding area. She was enjoying her freedom tremendously when she began to hear sublimely beautiful music, akin to the sound of wind chimes. She was then sucked (head first) into a tube, and although the tube was dark, she was aware that she was moving towards a light. As she emerged from the tube, the music she was listening to turned into hymns, similar to what she had heard during her first NDE.

At this point she found that she was surrounded by trees, flowers, and a vast number of people. The place was full of light, and everyone, including herself, was made of light. She also experienced a sense of profound love, as if love poured from even the grass, trees, and birds.

She then recognized five people who she had known during her earthly life. Reaching out, they welcomed her. Two of them, Vicki and Diana, were Vicki's blind schoolmates, who had died earlier. Two others had been her caregivers in childhood who had also passed away. The fifth person was Vicki's grandmother, who had recently died. In these encounters with her loved ones no words were spoken. She simply felt an overwhelming love and acceptance from everyone.

After that Vicki was flooded with information of a religious nature, as well as scientific and mathematical knowledge. She also intuitively received answers to every question she had ever had, including those concerning God. As these revelations were unfolding, she felt the presence of a figure whose radiance was far greater than her loved ones. Vicki identified this person as Jesus, who communicated with her telepathically.

She wanted to stay, but Jesus told her that it was not her time and that she must go back to her body to have children. Vicki was childless during her NDEs, and agreed to return to earth.

Before going back, however, Jesus showed her a panoramic survey of her life from birth. After her life review she felt and heard a "sickening thud," like a roller-coaster ride flinging her back into her body, in which she felt heavy and full of pain. It took her almost a year to fully recover from the accident. But since then, as she was promised in heaven, she has given birth to three children.

NEAR DEATH EXPERIENCES AND PSYCHIC ABILITY

During NDEs some people see future events which later become true. For example, as we have just seen, Vicki Umipeg was childless during her near death experience, but Jesus told her that she needed go back to earth to have children—which is precisely what occurred. Before this experience she was trying desperately to become pregnant, without success. One woman whose NDE occurred during childbirth, reported that she was telepathically told by a being of light to go back to give birth to her son, and that later she would raise him alone. Despite her wish to remain in the spirit world, she went back to her physical body and gave birth to a boy. One year later she was deserted by her husband.

In one study the authors reported that 40% of respondents who had near death experiences described a transcendental environment in which they wished to stay, but were forced to go back. Before their NDEs, 47% of the respondents believed in an afterlife while 78% had a fear of death. Afterward, however, 100% reported a belief in an afterlife based on their own experiences, which explicitly contradicted their previous views. Furthermore, none of the respondents reported any fear of death. According to this report, after having an NDE many people develop psychic abilities, while 92% feel more in touch with an inner source of wisdom and have a very strong sense of being guided.

Interestingly, four individuals (out of 40 studied) who were school librarians, office workers, and housewives before their NDEs, started to use their gifts and became psychic healers. Psychic abilities in these respondents include clairvoyance, precognition, dream awareness, healing ability, and perception of auras, along with other talents.[90] The psychic gifts they acquired, and especially overcoming their fear of death, indicate that NDEs are transcendental in nature and provide a glimpse of something beyond the physical world.

Calcutta (Kolkata), India, Amitava's birthplace. In this back street of the city sacred cows roam freely.

CAN HUMAN CONSCIOUSNESS SURVIVE PHYSICAL DEATH?

We cannot escape the obvious: human consciousness seems to be able to exist outside the brain. But how can we explain this in purely scientific terms?

Probably the brain has a filter which selectively provides certain information during waking consciousness. Under certain unknown or poorly known circumstances, however, this filter system may no longer work, drastically altering the normal mind-brain relationship, in turn

---

90. Sutherland C. "Psychic phenomenon following near death experiences: An Australian study." J Near Death Studies 1989; 8: 93-102.

causing enhancement of consciousness.[91]

Does the loss of our filtering mechanism predispose us for transcendental experience? The answer is not known. But there are quantum hypotheses of human consciousness indicating that the human mind is non-local (that is, it is a separate entity from the brain), and that during an NDE it may separate from the physical brain and become a part of the universe. However, if the person survives, human consciousness returns to the brain; if the person dies, his or her consciousness may remain in the universe (or another realm). I discuss this aspect in detail in Chapter 6.

If human consciousness has dualistic properties, like subatomic particles (wave-particle dualism according to the principles of quantum mechanics), then at death human consciousness may separate itself from the dead brain and go onto exist in another realm. Though from a purely scientific viewpoint the existence of human consciousness after death is still a hypothesis, it is just a matter of time before it becomes an established fact.

CONCLUSIONS

Since so many aspects of near death experiences cannot be explained by science, it is self-evident that NDEs strongly suggest, or in some cases even prove, the presence of an afterlife as well as the immortality of the soul—both which are part of the belief systems of all religions.

This is more than just a theory, and it is far more than mere wishful thinking or "whistling past the graveyard," as skeptics maintain. Both the world's great spiritual leaders and the faithful have always known what scientists are just beginning to discover: There is no such thing as "death." Life is an endless chain of experiences in which our soul cycles between wondrous and mysterious realms on its eternal quest for oneness with God.

---

91. Greyson B. Kelly EW, Kelly EF. "Explanatory models for near death experiences." In *The Handbook of Near Death Experience* (Holden JM, Greyson editors). Praeger Publishers, 2009, pp. 213-234.

TABLE 1
FEATURES OF PLEASANT NEAR DEATH EXPERIENCES

- Out-of-body experiences that may include seeing the physical body from above, listening to the conversation of doctors, witnessing medical resuscitation procedures performed on the body, and possibly hearing the doctor pronounce the person dead.
- Being in a pain-free calm state, with heightened senses and perceptions.
- An overwhelming feeling of joy, peace, and happiness.
- Being in a heavenly environment significantly more beautiful than earth, and witnessing non-physical beings.
- Going through a dark tunnel and seeing a bright but pleasant and inviting light at the end, then coming out into a beautiful earth-like place, but which is much nicer than earth.
- Altered time perception.
- Meeting with a self-luminous being of light (depending on religious belief it could be Jesus, Abraham, a Hindu deity, or an unidentified light being who is loving, caring, and wise).
- Deceased relatives and friends. Often deceased pets may be present.
- Seeing a border around heaven, or a point of no return between it and earth.
- A life review showing a person how their actions on earth affected others (often experiencing their responses as well), with emphasis often placed on good deeds rather than on the mistakes the person made.
- Some individuals say that their spiritual body (soul) is connected to their physical body by a stretchable cord (often attached between the shoulder blades, or sometimes at the solar plexis).
- At some point a person is told that his/her time is not up and he/she must return to their physical body.

TABLE 2
QUESTIONS IN GREYSON NEAR DEATH EXPERIENCES SCALE

- Did time seem to speed up or slow down?
- Did your thoughts speed up?
- Did scenes from your past come back to you?
- Did you suddenly seem to understand everything?
- Did you have a feeling of peace or pleasantness?
- Did you have a feeling of joy?

- Did you feel a sense of harmony or unity with the universe?
- Did you see or feel surrounded by a brilliant light?
- Were your senses more vivid than usual?
- Did you seem to be aware of things going on elsewhere as if you had ESP?
- Did scenes from the future come to you?
- Did you feel separated from your body?
- Did you seem to enter some other plane or unearthly world?
- Did you seem to encounter a mystical being or presence, or hear an unidentifiable voice?
- Did you see deceased people or religious spirits?
- Did you come to a border or point of no return?

Each question can be scored from 0 (no) to 2 (very positive response) and a total score of 7 indicates that the person has had a near death experience.

TABLE 3
COMMONLY REPORTED POSITIVE TRANSFORMATIONS IN INDIVIDUALS AFTER NEAR DEATH EXPERIENCES

- More loving and empathic towards others.
- More involvement with family members.
- Tolerance and acceptance of others.
- Higher sense of moral and social justice.
- Better understanding of purpose and meaning of life.
- Greater interest in religion/spirituality.
- Living a happier life.
- Better appreciation of nature and even ordinary things.
- No or little fear of death.
- Strong belief in afterlife and God.
- Overall better quality of life.

TABLE 4
SCIENTIFIC HYPOTHESES THAT ATTEMPT TO EXPLAIN NEAR DEATH EXPERIENCES

- Anoxia of the brain (absence of oxygen supply to the brain).
- Involvement of temporal lobe.
- Drug-induced near death experiences.

- Endogenous endorphins (morphine like compounds produced by the human brain) or neuro transmitter serotonin responsible for NDEs.
- Centripetal ischemia of the retina (reduced or lack of oxygen supply to the retina).
- Other neurobiological mechanisms.
- Psychological hypotheses.

TABLE 5
ASPECTS OF NEAR DEATH EXPERIENCES THAT INDICATE POSSIBILITY OF AN AFTERLIFE

- People of all ages (children to very old) may have near death experiences. Interestingly, the prevalence of NDEs in children who are not culturally or religiously primed are much higher than adults and their experiences are similar to adults.
- Children often gain information during NDEs, such as a deceased grandmother who they had not been aware of beforehand.
- Many aspects of NDEs are universal regardless of religion, gender, gender orientation, race, socioeconomic class, nationality, etc. Even atheists and agnostics have NDEs.
- Veridical near death experiences are NDEs in which observations are made or information is gathered by the experiencer that could not have been procured conventionally, and which can be verified by others later on. There is no known scientific principle that can account for this phenomenon, which strongly suggests that not only is consciousness separate from the brain but that it survives physical death.
- Near death experiences of blind people, including those blind from birth, are similar to the NDEs of sighted people.
- After their NDE most people no longer fear death. Moreover, they become kinder and more loving towards others. However, individuals who had similar life threatening illnesses but no near death experience, usually retain their fear of death and do not experience positive changes after recovery.
- According to traditional cultural and religious teachings, suicide is a selfish cowardly act and those attempting it are punished. However, many attempted suicide victims report positive NDEs.
- After near death experiences many people become more intuitive or may develop psychic abilities.

6

THE SOUL IS IMMORTAL: PAST LIFE MEMORIES

INTRODUCTION

Although the existence of God, immortality, and the soul traditionally belong to the realms of philosophy, theology, and religion, in the last 50-60 years papers have been published in mainstream scientific journals on topics such as near death experiences, cases of children who remember past lives, and death related sensory experiences. There has also been an increase in writings on the various aspects of parapsychology; for example, clairvoyance, precognition, telepathy, out-of-body experiences, transcendental experience, and others. Many people, including some scientists, now believe that NDEs are actual glimpses of the Afterlife.

According to the law of conservation of mass, matter can neither be created nor destroyed. It can only be transformed from one form to another. For instance, when a piece of wood is burned it appears that its mass is being totally consumed by the fire. In reality it is being transformed into various gases, including carbon dioxide and water vapor. If you accurately measure the mass of all these substances, you will find that they weigh exactly the same as the original piece of wood. This is the law of conservation of mass in action.

Another example is the generator, which converts mechanical energy into electrical energy. Einstein proved that mass can be converted into energy in his famous equation:

$$E \text{ (in Joules)} = m \text{ (in kilogram)} \times c2$$

E represents energy, m, the mass being converted into energy, and c represents the speed of light—which is expressed as 3×10^8 meters/sec. Therefore, when a very small amount of mass is converted into energy, massive energy is obtained due to the large value of "c." If one kilogram of mass is converted into energy, then it will produce 9×10^{16} Joules of energy, which is equivalent to 2.5×10^{10} KWh (250000000000 kilowatt hour). The average consumption of electricity by an American family is 10,000 KWh for an entire year. Therefore, if one kilogram mass is converted into energy it would provide electricity for a city with 250,000 families for ten years.

Classical laws of physics, such as the law of conservation of mass or energy, do not allow for the possibility of immortality of the soul. This is because when a corpse is cremated its mass is converted into other forms of matter, such as gases and residual ash. In the eyes of atheistic science, this marks the true end of that human being.

The spiritually aware, however, know that the soul (mind) is not physical but eternal, and that therefore it is not incinerated with the cremated body. Instead, because it cannot be destroyed only transformed, it moves on intact into another dimension. And in fact, quantum mechanics implies that human consciousness *does* live after physical death.

Quantum mechanics attempts to explain the behavior of subatomic particles where principles of classical mechanics are not applicable. In quantum mechanism a subatomic particle

The Hindu goddess Kali, whose name means "black," is an aspect of Mother Nature. Hence she is known as the great Creator, Preserver, and Destroyer of the Hindu pantheon. The wife of the god Shiva, Kali is closely linked with the Divine Feminine, Tantrism, creative power, and the primordial cosmic energy Shakti.

may be created or destroyed very fast, even faster than a fraction of a second. In the latter part of this chapter we will see how a scientist postulated the existence of consciousness or a soul using the principles of quantum mechanics.

CHILDREN WITH PAST LIFE MEMORIES

Although rare, some children describe their past lives in such detail that the information can be verified. Professor Ian Stevenson (1918-2007), a well-known psychiatrist who was the former chair of Department of Psychiatry and Carlson Professor of Psychiatry from 1967 to 2001, and then Research Professor of Psychiatry from 2002 until his death, founded the university's Division of Perceptual Studies, which investigates paranormal phenomena. Dr. Stevenson studied reincarnation using a survey of children who could remember their past lives, and collected approximately 3000 cases throughout the world. In his first scientific paper he reviewed 44 cases and postulated the possibility of reincarnation.[92]

Alexandrina Samona, the five year old daughter of Dr. and Mrs. Carmelo Samona of Palermo, Sicily, died of meningitis on March 15, 1910. A year later Mrs. Samona gave birth to twin girls, but one had an extraordinary resemblance to the first Alexandrina, and so they named her Alexandrina II. She even displayed behavior similar to her deceased sister.

At age eight her parents told her that they were going to visit Montreal, Canada. Alexandrina II said that she had visited that place before—although she had never been there in her present life. She told about going to a great church with a very large statue of a man with his arms wide open. She also recollected that there was a lady present during their trip, and that she had met a group of little red priests.

Her mother, Mrs. Samona, then recalled that she had indeed travelled to that place with Alexandrina I some months before her death, and that they had visited a church with a female friend. They had also met a group of young Greek priests wearing blue robes decorated with red ornaments. This type of evidence indicates that Alexandrina I

---

92. Stevenson I. "The evidence for survival from claimed memories of former reincarnation." J Am Society Psychic Res 1960; 54.

reincarnated as Alexandrina II.

Reincarnation can be defined as a phenomenon where after a person's death the physical body perishes, but the mind survives and later can inhabit another physical body.[93] (It is important to note that early Pagans as well as Christians, in particular Gnostic Christians, considered the human mind to be identical with what we call the human soul.)[94]

TYPICAL FEATURES OF CHILDREN WITH PAST LIFE MEMORIES

Most children with past life memories typically begin describing their past lives when they are very young (between 2 to 4 years old, though the average age is 37 months), but usually stop talking about them when they turn six or seven years old, the time when they start going to school. Some may make statements about past lives casually, while others may attach strong emotions and may beg or cry to see their previous families. The median interval between death and current birth (reincarnation) is 16 months.

In general, children with past life memories describe ordinary lives, usually in the same country. But one striking feature is that 70% of deaths in the previous lives were unnatural deaths. Interestingly, 75% of children with past life memories provided details of their deaths in their previous personalities, especially if the death was violent in nature, such as murder. In the case of a violent death in a past life a child may show anger towards its murderer and may often identify the offender.

Sometimes subjects report that they were previously a member of the same family, while others describe previous lives in some other place.

Cases with children with past life memories are easiest to find in cultures that believe in reincarnation, such as India, Sri Lanka, Thailand, and Myanmar. But cases are also found in Europe and North America. American parents are probably reluctant to talk publicly about their children having past life memories. Some children can recall past life memories on demand, while others require a certain frame of mind to access them. As children grow older they may totally forget their past life memories, although in cases where a previous personality has been

---

93. Cockburn D. "The evidence for reincarnation." *Religious Studies* 1991; 27:199-207.
94. Lochlainn Seabrook. *Jesus and the Law of Attraction*. Sea Raven Press, 2014, passim.

identified and two families keep in touch, past life memories may last much longer.

Although many children retain their gender from past lives, sex-change may also occur during rebirth (commonly found in Myanmar). The phenomenon of children with past life memories can be explained by the concept of reincarnation, but the process by which consciousness is transferred from a deceased person to a new body is completely unknown to science.[95]

BIRTH MARKS AND BIRTH DEFECTS IN SOME CHILDREN WITH PAST LIFE MEMORIES

Bodily malformations that are unusually large or otherwise unusual in shape or location occur rarely. However, malformations (skin abnormalities or substantial birth defects) occur frequently among children with past life memories. Sometimes a young child with this type of birth mark speaks about the life of a deceased individual who suffered a wound (most likely a fatal wound) that corresponds somehow with the birth mark of his/her present life.

Stevenson extensively investigated this intriguing phenomenon and found that among 895 cases, 309 (35%) of the children had large or irregular birth marks or malformations. Children of this group are found mainly in countries and cultures with a tradition of belief in reincarnation, but they also occur in Europe and in North America where families do not embrace this belief.[96] Pasricha et al reported malformations or birth marks in 12 cases where they were verified to be from previous lives. Let us look at two of their more intriguing cases.

Case Report 1: NK was born in the village of Kharwa, in Rajasthan, India, in 1981, with a linear area of abnormal skin on the left area of his head. Once, while still a toddler, after he was chastised he began walking away from his family's house. When asked where he was going, he said, "I am going to my village Sarina. My wife is Dakho and my son is Madan."

He rejected his current name and wanted to be called Babu. He

---

95. Tucker JB. "Children's report of past-life memories." *Explore*, 2008; 4: 244-248.
96. Stevenson I. "Birthmarks and birth defects corresponding to wounds on deceased person." J Scientific Exploration 1993; 7: 403-410.

talked about the life of Babu until he was 5 or 6 years old, and also said that Babu was killed by robbers, who had hit his head with an axe. The details corresponded to a man named Baby who was murdered in 1978. Although the distance between Kharwa and Sarina is only 6.5 km (4 miles), the family of NK did not know the family of Babu before this incident. However, they were aware of the murder.

Later, when this case was more rigorously investigated by one of the authors, it was discovered that a young married man named Babu, who was married with a child, lived in that village. He had a small tea shop in Sarina, and one day while walking from the store to his house he was murdered by robbers, who struck him on the head and elsewhere with an axe, and dragged his body to a nearby well. Two men were arrested for the crime but were later acquitted for lack of evidence.

The investigator reported that NK made 19 statements about the life and death of Babu, and of these, seven regarding Babu and his family could be verified. The remaining statements were about the killing of Babu, but the police report verified four additional statements regarding his murder. NK also spontaneously identified five members of Babu's family when they met. Based on a review of the postmortem report, the investigator verified that the skin anomaly on NK's head closely resembled Babu's fatal head wound.

Case Report 2: DG is an American boy born in 1997 with a birth defect in his heart (narrowing of the pulmonary artery near valves), but his mother reported no infection during her pregnancy, and no history of birth defects in the family. This is a rare problem that occurs only once in every 70,000 births. DG was treated for the defect right after birth, and he did well after that with no lifestyle restriction.

DG's birth defect was similar to a fatal wound suffered by his maternal grandfather (LS) during a shooting in 1992, which killed him. LS, a retired police officer, but working as a security officer at a bank, went to a store and discovered that a robbery was taking place. He pulled his revolver on the assailant at the cash register, but was unaware that there were others behind him. It was their gunfire that killed him. During the autopsy it was revealed that the bullet went through his chest and left a wound mark on his heart.

When DG was old enough to talk he made a number of statements indicating that he had knowledge of his deceased grandfather, which he could not have gotten through normal means. For example, when he was 3 years old and misbehaving, his mother told him to sit down, otherwise she would spank him. DG replied, "Mom when you were a little girl and I was your daddy, you were bad a lot of times but I never hit you." He later correctly described two cats that his family had, and even gave the correct nickname of one of them (which he had no way of knowing).

DG also talked about the death of LS as well as his personality, and said that several people were shooting during the incident. The investigator of this case commented that the narrowing of DG's pulmonary artery was a close match with the wounds of the pulmonary artery of LS. This case demonstrates that children with past life memories may also be born in the U.S., where reincarnation is not a common cultural or religious belief.[97]

INTRIGUING BEHAVIORS IN SOME CHILDREN WITH PAST LIFE MEMORIES

Many children with past life memories display behaviors that appear to be connected with the personalities of previous lives. For example, a child may show strong emotion towards the family members of his previous personality, and may act bossy towards the siblings he had in his previous life, although those siblings may be significantly older than the child in his/her present life. These emotions usually dissipate as the child grows older, but there are exceptions. Another common behavior is a phobia towards the mode of death of previous personalities. In fact, 35% of children with past life memories demonstrate this type of phobia. For instance, if a person drowned in a past life the reincarnated child may show a fear of swimming or being near water.

Stevenson and Keil investigated 750 children with past life memories in Myanmar (Burma), and 24 said they had been Japanese soldiers killed in Burma during World War II. However, unlike most Burmese children with past life memories, these 24 subjects could not remember the personal names or addresses of their previous personalities, and so these could not be verified.

---

[97]. Pasricha S, Keil J, Ticker JN, Stevenson I. "Some bodily malformations attributed to previous lives." J *Scientific Exploration* 2005; 19: 3: 359-383.

However, these same 24 subjects showed various behaviors, such as complaining about spicy Burmese food (asking for raw fish instead), dress preference, industriousness, and insensitivity to pain. These behaviors are uncommon among Burmese people, but were common among Japanese soldiers during the oppressive occupation of Burma. Knowing about the cruelty of the Japanese military during this period, it is unlikely that the parents of these children encouraged them to behave like Japanese soldiers.

Amitava's in-laws James Moore and Laverta Moore (left) and his parents (right).

Genetic factors cannot explain these behaviors because all of the children were born after 1945, and also because there were no Japanese soldiers in Burma after World War II. The authors suggested that the behavior of these subjects could not be explained by environmental factors either, and that a third factor must be present to account for it.[98]

Some children with past life memories often show an interest in addictive substances, such as tobacco or alcohol, if in their past lives they were addicted to them. For instance, there is the case of Sujith

---

[98]. Stevenson I, Keil J. "Children of Myanmar who behave like Japanese soldiers: a possible third element in personality." J Scientific Exploration 2005; 19: 171-183.

Jayaratne, whose neighbor obliged the young boy's requests for alcohol until his grandmother intervened.[99]

There are also reports of unusual play in children who claim to remember their past lives. Stevenson investigated 278 children who remembered their past lives, and observed 66 children (32.7%) who engaged in play that was unusual for their family, or who had no model among their family members or other obvious normal stimulus. However, their play habits corresponded to an occupation or some other aspect of their previous personalities.

The authors in this report verified that in 22 cases the child's play matched with the occupation or events in the life of a specific deceased person. In five of the cases the child's play was the first indication to parents that the child might be remembering his/her past life. Although occurring less frequently, some children engaged in play that was typical of the opposite sex, indicating that the gender can be switched between reincarnations. A small group of children named their dolls or other play objects after names they knew from previous lives. A few children reenacted the mode of deaths of previous deceased persons.

Sometimes the play of a child corresponds to the vocation of the previous life, such as pretending to be a shopkeeper, schoolteacher, nun, miller, well digger, garage mechanic, vehicle driver, physician, soldier, bandit, and others. One unusual finding was that some children pretended to sell pickled tea, a popular stimulant in Myanmar, suggesting that this may have been their occupation in a past life.

An interesting case is that of GN, who was born in a Brahmin family (highest caste in Hinduism) as the son of an Ayurvedic physician in Northern India. GN remembered his past life as a washerman belonging to a low caste. As a young child when GN observed his mother washing clothes, he not only wanted to help her wash them, but also iron them as well. This became such a nuisance that his mother had to discipline him. During playtime he pretended to be a washerman, and his mother would hear him saying, "My wife is sitting here cooking food and I am washing clothes."

---

99. Stevenson I. *Cases of the reincarnation type, Volume II, Ten cases in Sri Lanka.* University Press of Virginia, Charlottesville, NC, 1977.

Another intriguing case reported by Stevenson is that of CE, who was born in Middleborough, England. When he was able to speak, he remembered his past life as a German pilot during World War II, who died in a plane crash during a bombing mission. When he was between 2 and 3 years of age, he started drawing military insignias and badges. As he grew older his drawings got more detailed, and once he sketched an airplane with a swastika on it. He also demonstrated the Nazi salute with his little arm straight out. Later, when he started school and his classmates mocked him, he gradually stopped speaking about his past life.

Nearly all children who claim to remember a previous life as a person of the opposite sex, engage in cross-dressing when they are young children. For example, RK was a young girl in Sri Lanka who remembered a past life as a boy who had drowned in a well when he was a little over 7 years old. RK showed a preference for boy's activities, such as flying kites and playing cricket. She rode her brother's bicycle and climbed trees, totally unacceptable behavior for girls in Sri Lanka.

Sometimes children name objects or dolls after the names of the children they had in a past life. For example, HI was a young girl in Lebanon who remembered her past life as a woman named Wahed, who had five children. When her mother bought her a small toy coffee mill with three human figures on its top, HI named them May, Raja, and Samia, the names of three of her children in a past life.

In some cases a child may playact their death scene from a previous life. MS was a young boy from Myanmar who remembered the life of a man who drowned during a ferry accident. When MS was between 2 and 3 years old he would playact the scene of a man trying to escape from a sinking boat with his playmates.[100]

One question about children with past life memories is what happens to them between death and reincarnation. Approximately 20% of subjects report some memory between lives. Some children said they stayed near where their previous personality died, while many others described funerals or other activities in the family after their death. Some children talked about other realms and seeing other entities. But such reports, although fascinating, cannot be verified. The two cases of

---

100. Stevenson I. "Unusual play in young children who claim to remember previous lives." J Scientific Exploration. 2000, 14: 557-570.

American children with past life memories are also reported by Dr. Tucker.[101]

TWO AMERICAN CASE REPORTS

Case Report 3: Sam Taylor was born 18 months after his paternal grandfather died. When he was one and half years old he looked up at his father, while his diaper was being changed, and said that once he changed his father's diaper when his father was little. He eventually provided detailed information about his grandfather, information that his parents said he had no way of knowing.

For example, his grandfather's sister had been murdered, and his grandmother used a food processor to make a milkshake for his grandfather every day. When Sam was four and half years old his grandmother died and his father went to take care of the family estate. When Sam's father returned with family pictures, he correctly identified a photo of his grandfather. To test him, his mother showed him a class picture that included 16 boys. Sam was able to pick his grandfather out of the group.

Case 4: Kendra Carter started swimming when she was four and half years old, and immediately became attached to her female swimming coach. She began saying that the coach's baby died when he was very sick, and that she had pushed the baby out. Kendra's mother was always with her during swimming lessons, and when she asked Kendra how she knew this she replied that she was that baby. Kendra went on to describe an abortion. Her mother later found out that the coach had had an abortion nine years earlier. Kendra spent lots of time with her coach, even staying with her three nights a week.

Eventually the coach had a falling out with Kendra's mother and cut off contact with the family. Kendra went into a depression and did not speak for four and half months. At that point the coach reestablished limited contact with Kendra, and she slowly began talking and participating in normal activities again.

Usually the past life memories of children fade with time, they grow up to lead normal lives, and reincarnation researchers stop studying

---

101. Tucker JB. *Life Before Life: A Scientific Investigation of Children's Memories of Previous Lives.* St. Martin's Press, 2005.

them. However, there are a few followup studies dealing with children with past life memories after they enter adulthood.

In one such study the authors investigated 28 adults aged 28 to 56 years, who reported past life memories as children. Out of 28 subjects, 24 talked about some residual past life memories, while the other 4 did not recall any. Moreover, three out of the 24 subjects who talked about past life memories were not even sure if these memories were related to past lives.

Interestingly, of the subjects who claimed to have genuine past life memories in adult life, the mean number of statements made about past lives were only 4 compared to 30 made when they were children, indicating that past life memories recalled during childhood tend to fade with age. The authors also commented that they found no indication that childhood memories of past lives have any adverse effect on the development of these children into adulthood. All subjects studied reported living a normal adult life.[102]

PAST LIFE REGRESSION UNDER HYPNOSIS

Some individuals can remember past lives under hypnosis, but in my opinion children with past life memories offer more convincing proof of reincarnation, because there are reports that the very nature of hypnotic suggestion can affect one undergoing past life regression.

Pyun reported that a life identity can be created during hypnotic regression. The author selected a real historical person and a fictitious person as two past life identities. After hypnotic induction, past life regression suggestions were given to six subjects. In five out of six of them the same past life identity suggested during hypnosis was produced. The author concluded that it is quite simple and easy to manipulate past life identity.[103]

In another study the authors observed that past life regression depends on the hypnotizability (not all subjects can regress to a past life under hypnosis) of a person, as well as their cultural and religious background. For instance, in a Canadian study all the subjects reported

---

102. Haraldsson E, Abu-Izzedin M. "Persistence of past life memories in adults who in their childhood claimed memories of a past life." J Nerv Ment Dis 2012; 200: 985-989.
103. Pyun YD. "Creating past life identity in hypnotic regression." Int J Clin Exp Hypn 2015; 63: 365-372.

to be humans in their past lives, while in a Korean study some subjects selected animals as their past life identities.[104]

Nevertheless, some practitioners believe that past life memories can affect one's present life behavior, and that past life regression therapy under hypnosis may resolve such issues.

Lucchetti et al described a case of a 38 year old male where suggestive past life memories were related to an unusual medical condition in his present life. The subject underwent past life regression therapy and remembered being a priest who had committed suicide with a crucifix nailed to his chest, and a medieval weapon (skull flail) hitting his cervical and left back region. In the present life he had an isolated obstruction of the right coronary artery and other medical conditions which showed an intriguing similarity with his past life wounds.[105]

Brian L. Weiss, M.D., a graduate of Columbia University and Yale Medical School, is considered a pioneer in past life regression research. In 1980 Weiss, head of the psychiatry department at Mount Sinai Medical Center in Miami Beach, treated Catherine, a 27-year-old woman suffering from anxiety, depression, and various phobias.

When Weiss hypnotized her she remembered repressed childhood traumas, and after that, during many other sessions, she provided compelling descriptions of a dozen or so of her hitherto unknown 86 past lives, as well as philosophical messages channeled from "Master Spirits." Catherine's anxieties and phobias soon disappeared and she was able to end therapy. Dr. Weiss later wrote his bestselling book *Many Lives, Many Masters*, based on his experience with Catherine.[106]

DEATH RELATED SENSORY EXPERIENCE

Dying children and adolescences with cancers sometimes report seeing people or religious figures (children often see angels, but without wings) that others cannot see. Often following such a sighting, which is called "death related sensory experience," children are at peace.

---

[104]. Pyun YD, Kim YJ. "Experimental production of past life memories in hypnosis." Int J Clin Hypn 2009; 57: 269-278.
[105]. Lucchetti G, dos Santos Camargo L, Lucchetti AL, Schwartz GE et al. "Rare medical conditions and suggestive past life memories: a case report and literature review." *Explore* (NY): 2013; 9: 372-376.
[106]. Weiss BL. *Many Lives, Many Masters: The True Story of a Prominent Psychiatrist, His Young Patient and the Past Life Therapy That Changed Both Their Lives*. Fireside, 1988.

More interestingly, some parents reported that they did not tell their child about his or her imminent death. For example, Nathan was five years old in 1998 when he was diagnosed with leukemia. His father reported that in 1999, when they were leaving the hospital, Nathan said that God was coming and that he was more excited to go to heaven than Florida. Going to Florida had been his make-a-wish trip. At that time Nathan did not know that he was going to die, but the experience gave both him and his parents peace of mind. Sometimes during a death related sensory experience a person may see a messenger whose purpose is to guide the individual in his or her journey through death to another realm.[107]

Not only children but also adults may have death related sensory experiences. Death related sensory experience may occur hours, days, weeks, and even months before death. Adults may see dead relatives, deceased friends, religious figures, and glimpses of heaven. Common features of death related visions are listed in Table 2. Approximately 10% of all dying people are conscious shortly before death, and among them 50 to 60% may experience deathbed phenomena, indicating that these kinds of experiences are common among dying patients who are conscious before passing away.

Death related sensory perceptions are most likely not hallucinations because dying people often report seeing a deceased person, while hallucinations are usually auditory in nature. Moreover, deathbed visions are veridical: often the dead person can be identified. Additionally, death related sensory experience has a profound spiritual and positive transformative effect both on the dying person and family members. Lack of fear of death is a striking phenomenon in dying patients after such experiences, because they express lack of fear both verbally and non-verbally, such as having calm facial expressions.[108]

As expected, death related sensory experience may occur among people of all cultures, religions, races, ages, genders, socioeconomic status, and educational levels. An Indian study reported that 40 families out of 104 reported unusual experiences and behaviors from dying

---

107. Ethier A. "Death related sensory experience." J Peadiatr Oncol Nurs 2005; 22: 104-111.
108. Mazzarino-Willett A. "Deathbed phenomenon: its role in peaceful death and terminal restlessness." Am J Hosp Palliat Care 2010; 27: 127-133.

persons. Thirty of these dying patients displayed behavior consistent with deathbed visions, such as interacting or speaking with deceased relatives, most commonly deceased parents.[109]

In another study conducted in the Republic of Moldova, the authors observed that 41 out of 102 families interviewed reported unusual behavior in a dying person before death. In 37 dying persons, experiences were related to death related sensory experience, as these dying individuals reported seeing a dead relative or friend who communicated with them. The authors identified six themes conveyed by such experiences: support, comfort, companionship, reunion, prognosis, and choice and control.[110]

MEDIUM AND AFTER-LIFE COMMUNICATIONS

Afterlife communications are usually performed by a medium who has extrasensory perception, allowing them to communicate with the deceased. There are two types of mediums: mental and physical. In general, a mental medium communicates with a deceased person through interior vision or hearing. It is also possible that the spirit of a deceased person may take over some activities of a medium, such as speech and or writing ability. A physical medium may communicate with the spirit through extrasensory perception, and the spirit is often physically present in the vicinity of the medium.

There are reports of independent voices, rapping sounds on walls, and movement of objects during communication between a physical medium and a dead person. A psychic may be different from a medium in that a psychic provides information to his/her client (sitter) about their life and future, as well as about the living and the dead. However, a psychic can also be a medium.

Sometimes bereaved individuals report seeing, hearing, or feeling the presence of a deceased person. This experience may profoundly affect their belief in the Afterlife and their attitude towards life and death. Scientific studies also show that such encounters have

---

109. Muthumana SP, Kumari M, Kellehear A, Kumar S et al. "Deathbed visions from India: a study of family observations in northern Kerala." *Omega* (Westport) 2010; 62: 97-109.
110. Kellehear A, Pogonet V, Mindruta-Stratan R, Gorelco V. "Deathbed visions from the Republic of Moldova: a content analysis of family observers." *Omega* (Westport)2011; 64: 303-317.

profound spiritual and healing effects on bereaved individuals.[111] In 2011, after the death of my dad, my wife had a vivid experience of seeing him wearing a white shirt, his favorite color.

Mary anoints the feet of Jesus with spikenard then wipes them with her hair, a mystical biblical portrayal of the "Holy Union" between the Divine Masculine and the Divine Feminine, known in Hinduism as Tantra.

Scientific research also indicates that receiving a reading from a gifted medium about the deceased is helpful during mourning.[112] However, it is important to find a genuine medium, because a fraudulent medium may give a nonspecific or vague reading (cold reading) using general statements, such as "I see your grandfather in spirit and he has white hair, and he says he loves you." This is true for everyone because we all have a grandfather. Sometimes a bogus medium fishes for information from the client or provides an arbitrary selection of statements that are over-interpreted by the client due to grief or wishful thinking. For instance, a statement like "your mother says she loves you very much, and she will protect you from heaven," is true for all deceased mothers.

Scientific papers involving research on mediums report mixed results. O'Keefe and Wiseman cite a study where five professional psychic mediums did readings for five sitters for a total of 25 readings. The mediums and sitters were visually and acoustically isolated from each other. After the readings the sitters were sent a list of statements from all the readings and were asked to evaluate them blindly. The results of the study did not support the existence of genuine mediumistic

---

111. Nowatzki NR, Kalischuk RG. "Post-death encounters: grieving, mourning and healing." *Omega* (Westport) 2009; 59: 91-111.
112. Beischel J, Mosher C, Boccuzzi M. "The possible effects on bereavement of assisted after death communication during readings with psychic mediums: a continuing bonds perspective." *Omega* (Westport) 2014; 70: 1690194.

ability.[113]

In another study a professional medium gave readings for seven absent sitters who had suffered losses connected to at least two people in their past. The medium was prevented from identifying the sitters. The sitters blindly evaluated all seven readings without knowing which reading was intended for which sitter. No sitter picked the correct reading and the overall results showed that the medium lacked the gift of communicating with the deceased.[114]

Schouten published a condensed overview of studies in which the statements of mediums or psychics were quantitatively evaluated. The major challenge was to determine if a significant number of correct statements deviated significantly from chance expectation, and if psi ability was necessary to explain the correct statements. The authors concluded that only a few studies reported significant positive results, but in these studies there were potential errors that might have influenced the outcome. Furthermore, they found that the majority of *accurate* statements made by psychics and mediums were by chance, and that their apparent successes indicate that it is the client who makes the psychic.[115]

This is not the whole story, however.

Other scientific studies provide scientific validity to mediumistic ability. Hafesteinn Bjorsson, a psychic medium from Iceland with the ability to see dead people in an apparent state of wakefulness, was tested by investigators. In one study he was asked to read 10 sitters in random order, and the sitters were brought in one at a time. During the reading he was visually separated from the sitter by an opaque curtain. In addition, the sitters were acoustically separated from the medium using earplugs and music piped through headphones.

Bjorsson's responses for each sitter were recorded. Later all the sitters were given all the reports unmarked, and were instructed to pick the readings they believed were intended for them. Four sitters

---

113. O'Keeffe C, Wiseman R. "Testing alleged mediumship: methods and results." Br J Psychol 2005; 96 (Pt2): 165-179.
114. Jensen GG, Cardena E. "A controlled long distance test of a professional medium." Eur J Parapsychol 2009; 24: 53-67.
115. SchoutenSA. "An overview of quantitatively evaluated studies with mediums and psychics." J Am Soc Psychic Res 1994; 88: 221-254.

correctly identified their readings, while two others picked readings that were related to them in some way. Analysis of the proper names and other details given by the medium provided additional support that he had in fact identified persons described in relation to some of the sitters.[116]

Kelly and Arcangel conducted two research studies where mediums provided readings about a particular deceased person to a proxy sitter. The real sitters then blindly rated the readings in order to identify which one was intended for them. The first experiment was small, involving four mediums and 12 twelve sitters. The results were not significant. However, the larger second study involving nine mediums (who were given photographs of the deceased) and 40 sitters obtained statistically significant results.

Many sitters commented that the mediums could not have gotten this type of information by normal means. For instance, one sitter had a deceased brother who was called Mikey when young, Michael when he was growing up, and finally Mike in his adult life. The medium accurately referred to him as Mike, Mikey and Michael. Another medium saw an elephant with its trunk up in the air sitting on a table. The sitter stated that his deceased wife had a ceramic elephant with an upraised trunk on a table among her collections. The authors commented that gifted mediums do exist. But like any talented person, they are rare and those who can perform positively under the rigorous conditions required by science are even rarer.[117]

Beischel and Schwartz conducted an experiment using a novel triple blind protocol involving eight University of Arizona students who served as sitters (four had experienced the death of a parent, the other four were a peer group who had suffered no personal losses). The authors recruited eight gifted mediums who had previously demonstrated psychic abilities in a laboratory setting. The sitters were not present during the readings and the mediums were blinded to the identities of the sitters as well as the deceased.

---

116. Haraldsson E, Stevenson I. "An experiment with the Icelandic medium Hafesteinn Bjorsson." J Am Soc Psychic Res 1974; 68: 192-202.
117. Kelly EW, Arcangel D. "An investigation of mediums who claim to give information about deceased persons." J Nerv Ment Dis 2011; 199: 11-17.

The authors observed significantly higher ratings for intended versus control readings. The results suggest that certain mediums can anonymously receive accurate information about deceased individuals, because the study design effectively eliminated all conventional mechanisms, as well as telepathy, as the source for obtaining this kind of data.[118]

For gifted mediums the question is, what is the source of the information they receive?

One obvious answer is from the deceased person, due to the survival of human consciousness after death. Other possibilities include clairvoyance, reading the mind of the sitter, or super-psi (retrieval of information via a psychic channel, the Akashic Record, or a quantum field). The actual mechanism remains unknown.

It is important to note that research in this field indicates that mediumship is not associated with conventional dissociative personality, psychosis, over active imagination, or any pathological condition of the brain. Moreover, many mediums are not in a trance state during their readings.

Delorme et al obtained psychometric and brain electrophysiological data from six individuals under a double blind condition. Each individual performed two tasks with their eyes closed. In the first task the participant was given only the first name of a deceased person, and 25 questions were asked. After each question the participant was given 20 seconds to silently perceive the information and then respond verbally. Responses were transcribed and then scored by individuals who knew the deceased person.

Of the four mediums whose accuracy could be evaluated, three scored significantly above that expected from chance alone. The correlation between the accuracy of the information and brain wave activity during the 20 seconds of silent mediumship communication was significant for frontal theta waves in one medium. Theta brain waves, which typically cycle at a rate of 4-7 times per second (4-7 Hz), are the second slowest type of brain wave and are observed in the early stage of sleep and dreaming. Theta waves have also been recorded during

---

118. Beischel J, Schwartz GE. "Anomalous information reception by research mediums demonstrated using a novel triple blind protocol." *Explore* (NY) 2007; 3: 23-27.

spiritual experiences or when the brain is in a highly creative state.

The authors also performed a second experiment. Combining these with the other results, they concluded that communicating with the deceased may be a distinct mental state that is totally different from ordinary thinking or imagination.[119]

CAN POPULATION GROWTH RULE OUT REINCARNATION?

World population is growing at an accelerated rate. A very rough estimate indicates that around 8000 BC, there were only 5 million human beings in the world, and by AD 1 there were approximately 300 million. However, the current world population is 7.4 billion, with an annual birth rate of 135 million and annual death rate of 50 million. The world population is increasing by 85 million per year, with a projected world population of 10 billion by the year 2050. Therefore, a common refutation of the hypothesis of reincarnation is that this hypothesis is inconsistent with population growth.

The obvious question is, where are all the new souls coming from?

One explanation is that animals are reincarnating as humans. Another theory is the traditional reductionist scientific explanation that there is no soul and that the human body is nothing but atoms and molecules. However, we must ask how it is that dead atoms and molecules are able to make a living human being? If we accept the concept of a soul that survives death and goes onto occupy another human body, then an apt analogy would be that the soul is the "driver" and the body is the "automobile."

There is a theory called the circular migration model that explains the phenomenon of population growth without discarding the reincarnation hypothesis. Here the number of human souls is constant: souls enter state A (the earth) from an undefined state B (another realm) through a process called birth. Souls then depart state A and return to an unknown state B through a process called death. Both birth and death are observable processes documented publicly through birth and death records. Assuming the total number of human souls is constant, then the

---

119. Delorme A, Beischel J, Michel L, Boccuzzi M et al. "Electrocortical activity associated with subjective communication with the deceased." Front Psychol 2013; 4: 834.

sum of incarnated souls living on earth (in state A) and un-incarnated souls living in another realm (in state B) should be the same throughout history. The question then is, how many people have lived on earth since the beginning of mankind? It has been estimated that from 50,000 BC to modern times, approximately 70 billion human beings have managed to survive into adulthood. If the number of humans beings who did not reach adulthood is added to this number, then the number exceeds 100 billion.

David Bishai commented that there is no way to estimate the exact number of human souls, and that the number may vary from a minimum number of 10 billion to a maximum of 100 billion. Therefore, population growth could simply be explained by reducing the dwelling time in state B (another realm) without rejecting the reincarnation hypothesis. Bishai calculated that the average dwelling time in state B (another realm) was roughly 543 years in AD 1650, but in AD 2000 it was 30 years.[120]

Based on the theosophical hypothesis, in general, the number of human souls in state B exceeds the number of human beings on earth. Purucker estimated that 50 billion souls are associated with earth.[121]

CAN PHYSICS EXPLAIN IMMORTALITY OF CONSCIOUSNESS OR THE SOUL?

Research on NDEs, children with past life memories, and to some extent after-death communication, indicates the possibility of survival of the human mind or consciousness after death. This is similar to the concept of the soul: after it leaves the human body it dwells in an unknown realm for an unknown amount of time and then occupies a new human body.

The existence of human consciousness (mind or soul) after the death of the physical body has not been established by rigorous scientific experiments, which is why there is a great deal of skepticism in the scientific community regarding any hypothesis that proposes this idea.

---

120. Bishai D. "Can population growth rule out reincarnation? A model of circular migration." J Scientific Exploration 2000; 14: 411-420.
121. G. de Purucker. *Fountain-Source of Occultism*. Theosophical University Press, 1974.

Moreover, using the materialistic reductionist approach of science (which maintains that reliable knowledge can only be gained by the five physical senses) toward the nature of the physical universe, it is impossible to prove the existence of human consciousness after physical death. Nevertheless, science is constantly advancing and, despite its many limitations, intriguing theories continue to be proposed by reputable scientists. One of them is the quantum hypothesis of the mind (consciousness).

Let us begin our examination of this theory with a short discussion on the connection between the mind and the soul.

In the 4th Century BC Plato argued that the soul occupies the *nous* (intellect) and that it is immortal. However, Plato's student Aristotle argued that an immortal soul cannot interact with a corporeal body. Aristotle instituted a new concept, stating that it is the mind which determines our speech, thinking, and remembering. In the 2nd Century AD Galen established that psychological capacities are associated with the brain. Descartes (1596-1650) argued that the incorporeal soul is identical to the human mind, and that it is not just concerned with reasoning, but also with perception and the senses.[122]

Quantum mechanics, which deals with the characteristics of atoms and subatomic particles, derives its name from the observation that some microscopic quantities can only change in discrete amounts (quanta) rather than in a continuous manner, as has been observed in macroscopic objects.

In general macroscopic entities follow classical mechanics, which was originally proposed by Newton in describing the three laws of motion. In contrast, these laws are not applicable to atoms and subatomic particles due to their wave-particle dualism. This dualism is hard to visualize because quantum mechanics is an abstract mathematical concept, and the uncertainty principle (the position of a subatomic particle) cannot be determined precisely. Although abstract in nature, quantum mechanics can shed light on the behavior of subatomic particles, which in turn relates to the question of the immortality of the soul.

When we consider that atoms and molecules are the building

---

122. Bennett MR. "Development of the concept of mind." Aust NZ J Psychiatry 2007; 41: 943-956.

blocks of all objects, our physical observation is not always accurate. For example, the human body appears solid to our eyes, but, in fact, 99.9% of it is empty space. This is because the building units of the human body are atoms, and most of the space inside an atom is empty.[123]

The human brain contains approximately 100 billion neurons which are linked to each other (synaptic connection), forming a complex network with approximately 100 trillion connections. Therefore, the human brain is actually a highly complex biological computer. Microtubules are hollow cylindrical structures in the cytoplasm (cytoplasm is a gel-like fluid inside each cell). Microtubules are formed due to the tubular aggregation of protein subunits. Microtubules are very small subcellular components (approximately 50 micrometers; one micrometer is one thousandth of a millimeter) present in almost all types of cells, including neurons. Microtubules serve as major architectural elements within the structural parts of neurons (axons and dendrites).

In 1995 eminent British physicist Sir Roger Penrose and American anesthesiologist Stuart Hameroff first proposed the "quantum theory of consciousness" (orchestrated objective reduction of the quantum state). According to this view, known as OrchOR, consciousness depends on a biologically orchestrated coherent quantum process in collections of microtubules within brain neurons, quantum processes that activate neurons. Moreover, the brain waves recorded by EEG (electro-encephalograph) may be related to warm temperature quantum vibrations in microtubules that are inside brain neurons. Consciousness is dualistic in nature: it can interact with the brain and also with the universe at the same time. Therefore, consciousness is a non-local entity, for it is not completely localized in the brain.

During near death experiences microtubules lose their quantum state, but the information in them can survive because it is diffused in the universe. If a patient is revived, then this quantum information can return back to the microtubules. If a person is dead, then the quantum information survives outside the human body in the universe

---

123. Alejandro Safie. "We are mostly empty space." http://expandyourawareness.net/empty-spce.html. Accessed June 15, 2015.

indefinitely.[124] This consciousness can also be defined as the human soul, which makes it immortal. However, there are many skeptics in the scientific world who challenge the validity of this theory. For example, McKemmish et al concluded that the OrchOR model is not a feasible explanation for the origin of consciousness.[125]

When were souls created?

Dr. Fred Alan Wolf theorizes that the soul emerged during the Big-Bang approximately 15 billion years ago (scientifically speaking, the estimated age of the universe is 13.8 billion years). The universe and the human soul will continue to exist for 20, billion, billion (20,000,000 trillion) more years until the current universe is destroyed during the "Big-Crunch" (currently the universe is expanding, but at some point this expansion will cease and the universe will collapse into nothingness). I discuss the Big-Crunch in Chapter 7.

The human soul is not a *physical* entity. Therefore, it is not bound by physical laws, such as light, the fastest travelling object in the universe (note that there are particles, such as the tachyon, a hypothetical particle, that can travel faster than light). Travelling faster than the speed of light is called superluminal speed.

The great deity Shiva has his own sect, Shaivism, the second largest religious community in modern day India. He is a member of the Hindu Trinity Trimurti, the husband of Parvati, and the patron god of yoga.

During NDEs the soul travels from the material world, which operates at a speed less than the speed of light, into another realm (the spiritual world), which operates faster than light. Therefore, during this transfer from one world to another, a tunneling effect may take place,

---

124. Hameroff S, Penrose R. "Consciousness in the universe: a review of the OrchOR theory." Phys Life Rev 2014; 11: 39-78.
125. McKemmish LK, Reimers JR, McKenzie RH, Mark AE et al. "Penrose-Hameroff orchestrated objective-reduction proposal for human consciousness is not biologically feasible." Phys Rev E Stat Nonlin Soft Matter Phys 2009; 80 (2Pt1):021912.

which is observed by many individuals having NDEs.
At superluminal speed, a soul transferring into another realm is not bound by the constraints of time and space. Therefore, time can move both forward and backward, explaining the process of the life review that is common to many NDEs.[126] In a typical life review an NDEer is shown key past events in his life, and sometimes future events, and often "judgement" is passed on one's life by a group of light beings (known as the "day of judgement" in the Bible.)[127]

CONCLUSIONS

Scientific evidence based on studies of children with past life memories, past life regression, death related sensory experiences, and after death communication, indicate the possibility of survival of human consciousness after physical death. Human consciousness may also literally be the human soul, which after death dwells in an unknown realm and then occupies another human body through a process called reincarnation. Hypotheses on quantum mechanics of the soul indicate that unlike the human body, it is a non-local object with a dual character: the ability to interact with the physical (the body) and the spiritual (the universe).

According to the OrchOR theory, the human soul resides in the microtubules of the neurons in the brain, and after death dissociates from the physical brain, and travels to an unknown realm or remains in the universe. However, the reductionist approach of science dismisses this theory, and there are many skeptics who consider human consciousness to be merely the result of the action of neurons at the molecular level.[128]

---

126. "The soul and quantum physics," in *Experiencing the Soul, Before Birth, During Life and After Death*, edited by Jay Rosen, Hay House 1998; pp 242-252.
127. Matthew 12:36. In many cases the NDEer must judge his own life after the life review.
128. An interview with Dr. Fred Alan Wolf. www.fredalanwolf.com/myarticles/soul and death Q&A pdf. Accessed June 16, 2015.

TABLE 1
FEATURES OF CHILDREN WHO
REMEMBER THEIR PAST LIVES

• Children with past life memories begin describing them when they are 2 to 4 years old (mean age 37 months).

• Usually when children are 6 to 8 years old and start going to school, they stop talking about their past lives.

• Median interval between the death of a person and the rebirth of their soul in the body of a new child is 16 months.

• Children usually describe their previous lives as ordinary lives and reincarnate in the same country, sometimes not too far from their previous lives.

• 70% of deaths in previous lives were unnatural deaths, including murder.

• Some children have birth marks or birth defects that appear to match wounds, usually fatal ones, suffered in previous lives.

• Approximately 75% of children interviewed by different investigators provided detail descriptions of their deaths in previous lives, and even more if the previous deaths were violent.

• Some people show behaviors similar to past lives, even phobias. For example, in one study authors reported that 31 of 53 subjects who drowned in previous lives showed a fear of being in water.

• Some children described memories of events between lives, including going to another realm and seeing other entities; but this information cannot be verified.

TABLE 2
WHAT PEOPLE SEE DURING
DEATH RELATED SENSORY EXPERIENCE

• Only the dying person reports seeing a dead relative, deceased friend, a religious figure, or a glimpse of heaven (other realms); but others present cannot see anything.

• In the case of seeing a dead family member or deceased friend, the dying person may identify this person, and their identity can be verified (veridical experience).

• Children often report seeing an angelic figure, but without wings (although in rare cases wings are seen).

- Often a dying person encounters a spiritual guide (usually an unspecified light being or a deceased relative) who helps him or her cross over to the Other Side.
- Deathbed sensory experience may occur hours, days, weeks, or sometimes months before death.
- Approximately 10% of dying people are conscious shortly before death, and among them 50 to 60% may have a death related sensory experience.
- Death related sensory experiences occur among people of all cultures, religions, races, ages, genders, socioeconomic status, and educational levels.
- Death related sensory experience has a positive spiritual transformative effect: the dying person becomes calm, peaceful, or even elated, transformations that are witnessed by caregivers, family members, physicians, and nursing professionals.
- The deathbed experience has a soothing effect, both on the dying person and their family.

7

FINDING GOD

INTRODUCTION

When I was a child I asked my mother where God lives. She replied, "God lives in heaven and heaven is high up in the sky." I was seven years old when India and Pakistan were engaged in war, and I was afraid that a fighter plane flying at high altitude might hit heaven and injure God. How can an injured God run the earth and the universe? Probably earth and every lifeform on it would be obliterated. Mother assured me that heaven is located at a much higher altitude than any manmade aircraft can fly. I was still frightened.

When humans first landed on the moon (Apollo 11) I did not expect Neil Armstrong to find God there. In 1969 I was eleven years old and not so naive. At that time my atheist father told me that if there is a God He must live at the center of our galaxy, the Milky Way, which is 30,000 light years away from our solar system. Later, as a teenager, I found out that following Einstein's theory, if an object travels at the speed of light (186,000 miles per second, or 300,000 kilometers per second), it transforms into energy.

It takes about 8 minutes for sunlight to reach earth. One light year is the distance travelled by light in one year, which is approximately 6 trillion miles. Therefore, if my father's theory is correct, that God lives at the center of Milky Way, then he is 180,000 trillion miles from earth. Therefore, it is impossible to reach him at our present level of technology because our human engineered spacecraft Pioneer 10 has travelled only 8 billion miles in 30 years.

All religions claim that God created the universe and all lifeforms on earth. Now we know that there are many stars in our galaxy that have planets, and some of these planets may be earth-like in nature. Therefore, the universe is probably full of life. If God is the creator of the universe and eternal in nature, he must exist outside the universe. Therefore, God is not restricted by space and time.

Moreover, God could not be a limited human, because then he would not be able to be everywhere in the universe at the same time (omnipresence). However, the human form may be his favorite because he created humans in his own image.[129] Infinite God has the capability to manifest anywhere, and when he shows himself to us he may take any form, appearing, as Meher Baba accurately noted, "to each individual according to what that person thinks God is."[130]

THE BIG BANG THEORY AND CREATION OF OUR UNIVERSE

Since God created the universe there must be a connection between God and its beginnings. In the scientific community it has long been accepted that the universe was born in a single violent event called the Big Bang. There was no concept of space and time before the Big Bang because the entire universe was constrained in a single point in space.

This revolutionary theory originated from the discovery by Edwin Hubble in 1929 that galaxies outside our own Milky Way are moving further away, each at a speed proportional to its distance from us—indicating that the universe is expanding at an extremely rapid rate. Hubble was studying the electromagnetic radiation of galaxies and discovered a phenomenon called "red shift," meaning that the distribution of the various wavelengths shift into the red region of the spectra (red has the longest wavelength in the visible region of the electromagnetic radiation, while blue has the shortest wavelength). Therefore, red shift indicates an expanding universe while blue shift suggests a contracting one.

Hubble quickly realized that there must have been a moment in the history of the universe when space and time were "crunched" together in a single point (depicted in many ancient religions as some form of "primordial egg"). The universe was extremely hot, which is

---

129. Genesis 1:27.
130. Meher Baba. *Life At Its Best*. E. P. Dutton, 1957, p. 3.

Hinduism possesses many of the same figures, rituals, creeds, symbols, stories, myths, art, and even words that Christianity does. Both even teach the esoteric doctrines of reincarnation and astrology. Each offers a legitimate path to the One Supreme God known as Brahma to Hindus, Jehovah to Christians.

what caused the Big Bang. Seconds afterward the temperature of the universe reached around 10 billion degrees. There were no atoms or molecules. Just a variety of fundamental particles and photons (light particles). Atoms and molecules were created from these fundamental particles (such as neutrinos, protons, electrons, etc.) when the universe started expanding and cooling off.

In the beginning the universe was opaque because free electrons scattered photons all over. But as atoms and molecules were formed, the universe became transparent. However, some ancient photons, the "afterglow" just after the Big Bang, can be observed today as cosmic background radiation.[131]

Stars started forming when the universe was 200 million years old. The present age of the universe is approximately 13.8 billion years (13.77 billion years to be more precise), based on data sent back to earth by NASA's Wilkinson Microwave Anisotropy Probe. Our solar system is approximately 4.5 billion years old, though humans have existed on earth for only a few million years[132]—just a fraction of geological time.

WHAT IS THE FATE OF THE UNIVERSE?

No one knows the real fate of the universe, but there are many possibilities. According to the "Big Crunch" theory, the expansion of the

---

131. One way to hear this "afterglow" is to turn on an old cathode ray tube (CRT) TV and set it to an empty channel. One will see a "snowy" screen and hear a din of white noise, the cosmic background radiation left over from the Big Bang.
132. NASA: WMAP. "Age of the universe." http://map.gsfc.nasa.gov/universe/uni_age.html. Accessed June 25, 2015.

universe will eventually stop and gravity will pull all of the galaxies back together, eventually collapsing inward. Therefore, at the end the universe will be a single black hole (matter so highly dense that not even light can escape from it due to its incredibly powerful gravitational pull).

However, the universe is expanding at a much faster rate than expected, indicating that something must be pulling galaxies apart from each other. This unknown force is called "dark energy." It has been speculated that dark energy (which we know very little about today) will eventually determine the fate of the universe. Our visible universe (all matter, including all the stars in all galaxies, planets, etc.) represents only 5% of the universe, while 27% of the universe is made of dark matter (which we cannot see), and 68% of it is dark energy.[133]

Because dark energy is the cause of the expansion of the universe, one day this expansion will tear it apart, a hypothesis known as the "Big Rip." In this scenario the gravity that holds the galaxies together will one day no longer be able to do so: the universe will be infinite in size, and at the last moment even atoms will disintegrate.

Currently we live in stelliferous age (an age full of stars which originated when the universe was 150-200 million years old). However, all stars (which are actually suns similar to our own) have a finite lifetime. This is because the hydrogen supply of a star (stars shine due to nuclear fusion between two hydrogen atoms producing helium) will eventually run out. The smaller the star the longer its life span.

For example, a star that is double the size of our sun has a life span of approximately 1 billion years, while the life span of our sun is approximately 10 billion years (our sun started glowing about 4.5 billion years ago and will glow for another 4.5 billion years, then die out, taking all lifeforms on earth with it).

The smallest possible star has 0.08 times the mass of our sun, and the smallest stars have an expected life span of 10,000 billion years. However, one day all stars will burn out, but not until the universe is approximately 10^{14} years old (that is, 100 trillion years old). Then a new age, called the "Degenerating Age," will begin. This age will be a dark age indeed: there will be no stars shining in the night sky, since by then

---

133. "Dark energy, dark matter," NASA science. http://science.nasa.gov/astrophysics/focus-areas/what-is-dark-energy/. Accessed June 25, 2015.

they will have all collapsed into black holes (the "Black Hole Era"). Black holes emit small amounts of radiation known as "Hawking's Radiation." Eventually, after 10^{100} years, there will be nothing left because every black hole will disappear. Photons, neutrinos, electrons, and positrons will simply roam around in a dark cold universe.[134]

According to the "Big Chill" theory, our universe will keep expanding until the vast majority of stars die and the universe becomes dark and cold (with the temperature reaching absolute zero: -2730° C. or -4600° F.). This end-of-the-universe theory is also called the "Heat Death Hypothesis."

There are some encouraging possibilities, however, one being the "Big Bounce Hypothesis." It predicts that one day the universe will collapse, but just before it does it will expand outwardly through a new Big Bang, and a new universe will be created from the old one. This indicates that the universe is oscillating between expanding, contracting, and then expanding again, and that there is no beginning or end. Just God, the universal "Alpha and Omega."[135]

Hindu religious texts also point towards this type of oscillating universe, wherein one is destroyed and a new one is created. Thus, the universe is birthless and deathless, and is merely cycling through periods of creation and destruction.

THE MULTIVERSE OR PARALLEL UNIVERSE MODEL

Although quantum mechanics is accepted as the only way to understand the behavior of atoms and subatomic particles, the basis of quantum mechanics, the Schrödinger's wave equation, predicts that subatomic particles, such as electrons, evolve into a weird state of "superposition"; meaning an electron can be in two places at the same time. However, in the real world this is not possible because I cannot be at home and work at the same time. I can either be at home or at work. However, my body is entirely made up of electrons, protons and neutrons, so why can I not be in two different places at the same time?

One explanation is the "Copenhagen Interpretation," proposed

---

[134]. Fred C. Adams, Greg Laughlin. *The Five Ages of the Universe: Inside the Physics of Eternity.* Free Press, 2000.
[135]. Revelations 22:13.

by Niels Bohr (discoverer of atomic structure) and Werner Heisenberg (discoverer of the Heisenberg Uncertainty Principle), which indicates that the weird state of subatomic particles collapses when we try to measure them. As a result we cannot see this phenomenon.

But in 1957 Hugh Everett published a paper indicating that when you encounter an object of superposition here and there, it splits you into two copies of yourself: one that can see the object "here" and another which sees it "there." Everett claimed that quantum mechanics reveals a new model of the universe that perpetually splits into "many worlds" co-existing side by side (multiple parallel worlds). Therefore, the universe we see is a tiny facet of a much larger multiverse containing many universes. In other words, everything in this universe, including all the galaxies, has a counterpart in another universe.[136]

Cosmologist Max Tegmark proposed four levels of parallel universes, which he explained in an article published in the May 2003 issue of *Scientific American*.[137] According to Tegmark, there is a person who is not you, but who lives on a planet called earth with a sun and eight other planets, just like our earth. Although the life of that person is identical to your life, they can decide not to read this book, while you have decided to read it. However, you will never see your twin in another universe. Space is flat and infinite and we can only see objects up to 14 billion light years away, an area called the "Hubble Volume." We cannot communicate with this universe, known as a Level I universe, because it is beyond our cosmic horizon. Yet the same laws of physics apply there as they do in all parallel universes.

Level II universes were created as a result of the inflation of bubbles due to an extremely rapid expansion after the Big Bang. Our universe is one of such bubbles, and other bubbles represent other universes. However, it is impossible to contact parallel universes because these bubbles are moving away from each other too fast.

Tegmark's Level III universe is a many-worlds interpretation based on quantum mechanics. In this model, when I am going left, some other me (in a parallel universe) is going right; but we do not have any

---

136. Buchanan M. "Many worlds: see me here, see me there." *Nature*, 2007; 448:15-17.
137. Tegmark M. "Parallel universes: Not just a staple of science fiction, other universes are direct implication of cosmological observations." *Scientific American*, May 2003; 41-51.

knowledge of one another. However, all of these parallel universes coexist in the same infinite-dimensional Hilbert's space (methods of expanding of algebra and calculus from the two-dimensional Euclidean plane and three-dimensional space to spaces with finite or infinite number of dimensions). This is the model most often used in science fiction.

A Level IV universe is more or less a mathematical concept. The laws of physics which govern nature are applicable in Level I, II and III parallel universe models, but physical constants may vary (for example, value acceleration due to gravity) in other universes. In contrast, in a Level IV parallel universe the laws of physics of our universe are not valid.

STRING THEORY AND MULTIPLE DIMENSIONS

Quantum mechanics can explain the behavior of subatomic particles while the relativity theory (the general and special theory of relativity) is needed to explain the behavior of the cosmos. Physicists are trying to combine quantum mechanics with the theory of relativity in order to formulate one theory capable of explaining everything. Einstein dedicated much of the latter part of his life to trying to come up with this theory. More recently the proposed string theory has sought to combine both theories into a single "Theory of Everything."

According to quantum mechanics, subatomic particles such as electrons, protons, neutrons (fundamental particles), etc., are the building blocks of all atoms, which combine together to form a molecule. However, according to the string theory the basic fabric of the universe is not fundamental particles, but infinitely thin strings which have length but no other dimension (a one dimensional string). These strings, also known as "superstrings," may have ends but may join up within themselves to form a loop.

Just as the strings of a guitar can produce many different melodies based on the vibration of the strings, different vibrations of superstrings can produce different fundamental particles, the building blocks of the universe. Therefore, we could say that this universe is nothing but melodies being played by superstrings, with one vibration manifesting as an electron and another as a proton.

The number of possible vibrations of superstrings is infinite. As expected, a superstring is very small in size, occupying the Planck length (10^{-35} m) and vibrates at specific resonant frequencies.[138] A superstring is significantly smaller than an atom (hydrogen atom: 10^{-10} meter). Therefore, if a hydrogen atom represents our solar system then a superstring is my cat Thor sitting on a chair in our house here on earth. The formulas that result from string theory predict more than four dimensions in space and time for consistency of mathematical equations (10 or 11 dimensions in the most common variants, though one version requires 26 dimensions), but extra dimensions are super-condensed within the Planck length.

Edward Witten combined five different string theories and proposed the M theory (requiring 11 dimensions), which also introduced the concept of brane.[139] This cosmological model indicates that our universe is entirely restricted to a brane (membrane) within higher dimensional space time called "bulk." It is possible that there are other universes also restricted to their individual brane, but which are moving through the bulk and interacting with our universe.

Additional dimensions may also be crunched up. This model can explain weak gravitational force compared to other forces; for example, the electromagnetic force. The reason is that gravity can leak through the brane (membrane) which surrounds our universe into the bulk.

Another interesting hypothesis of string theory is that it proposes the existence of a 10 dimensional universe before the Big Bang. During the Big Bang this 10 dimensional universe was split into a four dimensional and a six dimensional universe. We live in the four dimensional universe, which is expanding, while the other half (the six dimensional universe) is "crunching" down to a very small size.

Moreover, it is also possible that we live in a four dimensional universe that is restricted by a brane within a multidimensional universe that we cannot see. However, if we could reach the fifth dimension we could see another world that is different than our own, and be able to travel back in time. Interestingly, if we could reach the tenth dimension we might discover a wonderland. The reason is that, according to string

---

138. Nicolai H. "String theory: back to basics." *Nature*, 2007; 449: 797-798; Greene BR, Morrison DR, Polchinski J. "String theory." Proc Natl Acad Sci Use 1998; 95: 11039-11040.
139. Witten E. "Quantum mechanics of black holes." *Science*, 2012; 337 (6094): 538-540.

theory, superstrings vibrate in the tenth dimension and there is nothing beyond the tenth dimension.[140]

GOD, BIG BANG, STRING THEORY, AND HINDU RELIGION

God is eternal and created everything, not only our universe, but all other universes, including all living matter. Therefore, God must have existed before the Big Bang. The teachings of the Vedas are consistent with the "Big Bounce" hypothesis, which predicts that one day our universe will collapse. But before that it will expand outwardly through a new Big Bang, and a new universe will be created from the old one. Thus, there must be another universe that collapsed before the Big Bang, and which created the universe in which we currently live.

One day our universe will disappear, and then through another Big Bang a future universe will be created. The death of one universe is like Autumn, the season in which trees shed all their leaves and become bare; but in Spring new leaves grow, bringing the trees back to their original shape. This is a cyclic process. Though eventually all trees die, this is not true of the universe, for it has no beginning and no end. Only cycles of birth and death. Therefore, God is eternal: when one universe collapses he creates a new one.

This Hindu illustration is pregnant with spiritual motifs and symbolism for those, whatever their faith, who have "eyes to see."

The Hindu Puranas provide an interesting time frame for the cycle of the creation of a new universe and its eventual destruction.

According to the Rig Veda, at the beginning there was nothing and it was dark. No one knows what this period was like, only that there were no gods or goddesses; just a single supreme God. According to one

---

140. Rob Bryanton. *Imagining the Tenth Dimension: A New Way of Thinking About Time and Space.* Trafford Publishing, 2006.

verse, the universe originated from a single point (Sanskrit, *bindu*) and then expanded rapidly. Some liken this to the "primordial egg" that exploded during the Big Bang. Another verse says that the universe was created from *Hiranyagarbha* (a Sanskrit word meaning "golden womb"). Alternatively, *Hiranyagarbha* may represent Brahma, who was created by the supreme God Brahman.

Brahman, the eternal supreme God, is beyond our comprehension, but Brahma has a life span of 100 Brahma years. Brahma is the creator of the present universe in which we live; Vishnu is the preserver (or savior); and Shiva will be the destroyer of the current universe. The combination of Brahma, Vishnu, and Shiva is often called *Trimurti* (a Sanskrit word meaning "three heads" or "three individuals"). Most religions possess some form of a trinity (often with two males and one female), an idea that predates the Christian Trinity (Father, Son and Holy Spirit) by many thousands of years. See Table 1 for descriptions of the supreme Hindu God and Trimurti.

Brahma's time frame is very different from our earthly concept of time. One Brahma day consists of 4.32 billion human years when he is awake, followed by 4.32 billion years when he is asleep. Therefore, combining Brahma's wake time and sleep time, one complete Brahma day is 8.64 billion human years. At the end of his wake time, when Brahma sleeps at night, creation (most likely referring to all lifeforms on earth rather than the entire universe) is destroyed by fire or water, an act known as *Pralaya* in Sanskrit. When Brahma wakes up the next day he creates every earthly lifeform again; then when he falls asleep everything is wiped out again.

Interestingly, during earth's history, there have been at least five ice ages: extremely cold periods when glaciers advanced even into warm regions, affecting lifeforms all over the globe.

While earth life seems to have originated in oceans approximately 3.5 billion years ago (as noted, the estimated age of the earth and our solar system is 4.5 billion years), the first proposed ice age occurred from 1,700 to 2,300 million years ago. Most likely ice ages transpire every 150 million years and cold temperatures may last up to 1 million years. The last ice age started 1.6 million years ago.

We presently live in an interglacial stage known as the Holocene Epoch, which started after the end of the last ice age known as the

Pleistocene, 10,000 to 20,000 years ago. Possibly there was a recent little ice age, sometime between the 17th and 19th Centuries, when the average temperature of earth was cooler than today and glaciers advanced into lands that had not been covered by ice before.

The exact cause of the oscillation of earth's climate between ice ages and warmer periods is not completely understood, but many factors, such as solar radiation, changes in the orbit of the earth, movement of tectonic plates, etc., may be contributing factors.[141] Oscillations of earth's climate from an ice age to a warmer period may be loosely interpreted as the wake and sleep time of Brahma, but the years stated in Hindu scriptures representing these cycles are totally wrong based on scientific theory (million versus billion years).

After 100 Brahma years, which is 311 trillion 40 billion human years, our present universe will be extinguished. Then another 311 trillion 40 billion years will pass, and the supreme God Brahman will create a new Brahma and a new universe will born. The only number stated in the Puran that has any resemblance to science is 4.32 billion years (one day of Brahma), because our earth is approximately 4.32 billion years old. However, according to Hindu mythology our universe is currently in the 51st Brahma year, indicating that it is 156 trillion years old. This is inconsistent with science because our own calculations state that it is 13.8 billion years old.

No one knows the exact life span of the universe, but it will take 100 trillion years for all the stars to run out of fuel, turning the universe completely dark. According to the Puran the universe will last for 311 trillion 40 billion years. However, a new universe will not be born until all the black holes disappear, and this will take another 10^{100} years. This number, called a "googol" (the number 10 raised to the power 100, written as a 1 with 100 zeroes after it), is very large, even compared to the total mass of the universe (estimated to be 10^{50} to 10^{60} kg). However, the overall concept described in the Puran—that the universe was created from a golden egg that will one day begin shrinking, eventually disappear, and give birth to a new universe—correlates with

---

141. Smart LD. "How many ice ages were there?" http://unmaskingevolution.com/11-iceage.htm. Accessed June 27, 2015; "The ice age (Pleistocene Epoch)." www.epa.gov/gmpo/edresources/pleistocene.html. Accessed June 27, 2015.

current scientific theory. This is also consistent with the concept of the supreme God who is eternal, with no known beginning and no known end. Another interesting feature of Hindu mythology is that after 311 trillion 40 billion years, at which time the universe will be obliterated, everything inside it will enter the god Vishnu, giving him gigantic form (Maha Vishnu). Every entity inside Vishnu will be unconscious until the birth of a new universe. If Maha Vishnu is considered a gigantic black hole, then everything inside him will be unconscious, for no information can escape a black hole (escape through the space around a black hole that is known as the "event horizon," described by Steven Hawking). However, the life span of this kind of massive black hole will be 10^{100} years, not just 311 trillion 40 billion years, after which a new universe will be born, according to Hindu mythology.

Some verses in the Rig Veda indicate that the sun and the rest of the universe is woven in strings. The dancing of Lord Shiva is sustaining the world, because this activity metaphorically represents the movement of subatomic particles. Alternatively, the dancing of Shiva (*Nataraj*) in a Hilbert space may be a manifestation of the vibration of strings that sustain the fabric of the universe. The universe is preserved as long as Shiva is dancing, and when in the distant future he stops the universe will end.[142]

The Aditya Vedanta, introduced by Hindu philosopher Adi Shankara (mid to late 8th Century), preaches that only the supreme God Brahman is pure existence, consciousness, and bliss (*Sat-Chit-Ananada*); and also that he is the absolute, impersonal, eternal, non-transforming, all-pervading, and only eternal entity in the universe. The universe we see is an illusion (*maya* in Sanskrit), or a dreamlike state caused by ignorance. The human soul is essentially a representation of the supreme God, and therefore is self-luminous. However, due to *maya* we cannot see our true self and duality arises (causing us to believe that human beings are different than God and separate from God). This is because *maya* blocks God from us like a cloud in front of the sun. When the cloud is removed the sun becomes visible.

---

142. Fritjof Capra. *The Tao of Physics: An Exploration of the Parallels Between Modern Physics and Eastern Mysticism*. Shambhala, 5th updated edition, 2010.

In real life we see ourselves as limited entities constrained by space and time. However, the supreme God Brahman is not constrained by space and time, and when, through the cycles of births and deaths, we remove the veil of *maya*, then our soul will transit to the highest plane where we will be reunited with God. This plane is called *Nirguna Brahamanlok* in Sanskrit, because it is devoid of feelings, such as joy or sorrow, and is beyond good and evil.

Because string theory states that the universe, and indeed all matter, exists due to the vibrations of superstrings, some scholars argue that the concept of the universe as an illusion is consistent with string theory. However, the eternal God cannot be made of the vibrations of string and, as a result, the human soul is not made of strings either; although the human body may be a manifestation of the vibration of strings.

The concept of non-dualism is unique to a particular branch of Hindu philosophy, but it should be remembered that there are many alternative Hindu philosophies that are based on dualism; that is, God and humans (or human souls) are different entities, and God is the only supreme entity in the universe. Here, the only thing humans can expect from God is love and forgiveness. The concept of non-dualism is very difficult to understand because in *Nirguna Brahamanlok* nothing exists except God, and when a pure human soul is dissolved in the vastness of God, it loses its identity as an individual.

This is like a human being made of salt attempting to measure the depth of the Pacific Ocean. Whenever he goes into the water to measure it he dissolves, becoming part of the ocean. As a result, he no longer exists as an individual. If I myself turn out to be made of salt, I will stand by the ocean and enjoy its tranquility rather than attempt to calculate its depth.

GOD IS NOT CONFINED BY SPACE AND TIME

God created our universe and he is omnipotent (all powerful), omnipresent (present everywhere), and omniscient (all knowing). I have used the word "he" to represent God because God is commonly referred to as he in monotheistic religions. Knowing the true nature of the omnipotent, omnipresent, and omniscient God, however, is beyond human comprehension. "He" could be an "it," a "she," or even something we have no word for.

A tantric refers to Shakti, the driving force of the universe, as "she" because one representation of her is the goddess Kali. But a Hindu who is a devotee of Lord Shiva or Lord Vishnu always refers to them as "he," and Brahma, the creator of our present universe, is also a "he." My mother is a devotee of Lord Shiva and in her world God is a "he." Interestingly, almost no Hindu worships Brahma, as there is only one temple in India, to my knowledge, dedicated to him.

There can be no doubt that God is beyond time and space, otherwise he would be confined by the natural laws of the universe in which we currently live. The next question is, whether God lives in a parallel world outside our universe, or in a much higher dimension than our four dimensional universe?

If God does not live in our universe, how can he have full control of it? Or more simply, how can he listen to our prayers and sometimes grant our prayers? God does not grant unreasonable prayers, such as, if I pray to win the lottery so that I can be lazy and quit my job, or take my wife on a world trip. I count my blessings everyday and look at life as being half-full rather than half-empty. In the latter part of this chapter, I will discuss my thoughts on where God lives.

John Allister published an article in which he argued that based on the teachings in the Bible, God must exist in a higher dimension, not a lower dimension, so that from the higher one he can reach everywhere at the same time. Moreover, God created time, so he must be independent of time.

However, all of this does not make God unreal, because what is most amazing about him is that he loves us so much he sent to earth the Eternal Second Person of the Godhead, Jesus, who for 33 years was confined within space and time for us.[143] I am in complete agreement with this concept.

AVATARS IN HINDUISM: A STORY SIMILAR TO NOAH'S ARK

In Hinduism the savior Vishnu descended to earth at least ten times as an *Avatar* (a Sanskrit word meaning "the descent of god on

---

143. Allister J. "God, space and time." www.hoshuha.com/articles/space.html. Accessed June 30, 2015.

earth"). However, according to Hinduism Avatars are born through a natural process and endure the same pleasures and pains experienced by humans. Moreover, Avatars may be animal, human, or mythological figures. For example, Rama of the Ramayana was an incarnation of Vishnu. Interestingly, some Hindu scholars argue that Buddha, who introduced the Buddhist religion, was also an Avatar of Vishnu. A future Avatar of Vishnu will be Kalki Avatar, who, it is said, will destroy everything on earth.

Another interesting story is that of Matsya-Avatar, in which Vishnu incarnated himself as a fish.

In very ancient times there was a king named Manu who was a devotee of Vishnu. One day when he was praying by the river, a small fish came into his hands, and just as he was about to throw it back, it begged the king to save its life. Feeling sorry for it, he put it in a jar of water. But soon the fish grew too big for the small container. The king then threw the fish back into the river, where it continued to grow. It finally became so large that he had to put it into the ocean.

The gigantic fish then revealed his true self to the king, and advised him to build a huge boat on which he was to take seven sages, the seeds of all plants, and one animal of each type, because a great flood would come in seven days.

When the rain started the king took everything onto the boat. As the ocean became rougher and rougher, the gigantic fish appeared, and the king tied it to the boat using the royal serpent Vasuki. Then the fish propelled the boat to a protected location near a big mountain, keeping them safe until the flood was over and a new era commenced.

This pre-biblical story, which itself derives from a far older universal flood myth common to the ancient East, was also adopted by the Hebrews, who transformed it into the biblical tale of Noah's Ark.[144]

WHY REVELATIONS HAVE OCCURRED ON MOUNTAINS

Mountains play an important role in spiritual progress. In India, many sages prefer to live near the Himalayan Mountains or in nearby caves. One of the holy cities in India, Haridwar, is located at the

---

144. Lochlainn Seabrook. *The Way of Holiness: The Story of Religion and Myth, From the Cave Bear Cult to Christianity*, Vol. 1 Sea Raven Press, unpublished manuscript.

foothills of the Himalayans, and many holy people live there. The founders of the major world religions, Moses, Jesus, and Mohammad, had their revelations on various mountains. Moses had his first encounter with God on Mount Sinai, while Jesus was transfigured "up a high mountain apart," identified as Mount Tabor or Mount Hermon, and appeared to Peter, John, and James in a cloud of glory. The Prophet Mohammad, while in solitude on Mount Hira, received the Quran by divine revelation from the Archangel Gabriel, the messenger of God.

Scientifically speaking, the high altitude in mountains may alter human physiology, thus preparing the human mind to receive divine messages. Mountaineers have long described the experience of feeling the presence of another being, hearing voices, emotional manifestations, and visual hallucinations, as well as autoscopic phenomenon (psychic illusory visual experiences defined by the perception of images of one's body or face within space, either from an internal point of view, as if an individual is watching his/her mirror image, or from an external point of view). Moreover, these kinds of experiences are often encountered when one is in solitude.

The Genesaic Flood story is patterned on much older universal flood myths that once circulated across the Middle East. One of these was the pre-Christian Hindu tale of Matsya-Avatar, more evidence that, as the Christian mystic Paul observed during his Mars' Hill Sermon, all religions worship the same Supreme Being.

Moses saw an angel in a burning bush. Peter, James, and John saw the transfigured Jesus and images of Elias and Moses. Therefore, high altitude may affect brain functions, thus facilitating the experience of a revelation.[145] Brugger et al suggested that the physical and emotional

---

145. Arzy S, Idel M, Landis T, Blanke O. "Why revelations have occurred on mountain? Linking mystical experiences and cognitive neuroscience." *Medical Hypothesis* 2005; 65:841-845.

stress endured during mountain climbing causes the release of natural opioids, known as endorphins, which act on the temporal lobe, predisposing the human brain to revelatory experiences. Moreover, prolonged stay in high altitudes in isolation may also alter the function of the prefrontal lobe, which may facilitate visions.[146]

In my opinion, however, the revelations of the founders of the major religions are not hallucinatory in nature, but real experiences that are not accessible to average people, or even highly developed spiritual people.

WHY THE NUMBER 7 IS SACRED

Interestingly, the number 7 has special significance, not only in the Bible but in other religions and cultures as well. God created the universe in six days and on the seventh day he rested. Therefore, creation was completed in seven days, making the seventh day, the day of rest, sacred.

In the bible there are seven graces, seven deadly sins, seven gifts of the Holy Spirit, and other sevens with significance. There are seven churches in the book of Revelations. In Judaism, Passover, the Festivals of Weeks and Tabernacles, and Rosh Hashanah (New Year), each last for seven days. The ancient Hebrews had seven names for God. In Buddhism there are seven means of ascent towards the spiritual center, which occurs in seven steps. The Prophet Muhammad said that Allah created seven heavens, one above another, and that the characteristics of the seventh heaven cannot be described by any human language. The Japanese have seven gods of luck. And so on.

In Hinduism the number seven (in Sanskrit, *sapta*) is also sacred. According to Hindu scripture there are 14 worlds in our universe, seven upper levels (Sanskrit, *urdha loaks*) including earth, and seven lower levels below the earth. The upper levels are layers of heaven, while the lower ones are various levels of hell. Moreover, there are the Sapta Rishis ("seven sages"), who are given special status in Hinduism due to their profound wisdom.

According to Hindu mythology, these seven sages represent the

---

146. Brugger P, Regard M, Landis T, Oelz O. "Hallucinatory experience in extreme altitude climbers." Neuropsychi Neuropsy Behav Neur 1999; 12: 67-71.

seven stars known as the Pleiades or Seven Sisters. In astronomy the Seven Sisters (Messier 45 or M45) is an open star cluster dominated by hot blue and extremely luminous stars located in the constellation of Taurus. One of the nearest star clusters to earth, its stars were formed approximately 100 million years ago.

Sapthapadi (a Sanskrit word meaning "walking seven steps") is a ritual performed during Hindu wedding ceremonies in which the bride and bridegroom walk seven steps in front of a sacred fire. Additionally, in Hinduism there are seven holy cities (Varanasi is the holiest), seven holy rivers (including the Ganges), seven seas, seven holy hills, and many other things relating to the number 7, making this number very hallowed in Hindu religion.

According to Hindu astrology, the 7th house is very important in one's astrological chart because it represents one's marriage. In tantric practice there are seven chakras or energy centers in the human body. Chakra means "spinning wheel" in Sanskrit. The Western and Sanskrit names for these chakras, along with their functions, are listed in Table 2. In numerology the number seven is associated with spirituality. If the birth number is seven, the person will seek spirituality in his or her life.

In quantum mechanics there are even seven principles. These principles include Hilbert space, measurement, time, space, composite system, the Bose-Fermi alternative, and internal symmetry.[147] Moreover, the color spectrum has seven colors, whose acronym is VIBGYOR: violet, indigo, blue, green, yellow, orange and red.

Finally, we have seven days in our modern week, each which was named after the sacred days of the seven primary gods and goddesses of ancient Europe. Beginning with the first day of the week, these are: Sol (Sun's day), Luna (Moon's day), Tiw (i.e., Mars, Tiw's day), Woden (Woden's day), Thor (Thor's day), Frig (Frig's day), and Saturn (Saturn's day).[148]

The sacrality and mystique of the number seven probably derives from the fact that the human head has seven holes in it, and the skull is associated with the seventh chakra, known as the Sahasrara Chakra. Also

---

[147]. Volovich IV. "Seven principles of quantum mechanics." December 2002, Cornell University Library. arxiv.org/pdf/quant-ph/0212126.pdf. Accessed July 4, 2015.
[148]. Lochlainn Seabrook. *The Goddess Dictionary of Words and Phrases.* Sea Raven Press, 2010, p. 27.

known as the Crown Chakra, it is in turn connected to what has been variously named Cosmic Consciousness, God Consciousness, Buddha Consciousness, Moses Consciousness, Christ Consciousness, etc. Thus Jesus is said to have been crucified on Golgatha, "the place of the skull."[149] The "golden bowl" is another mystical biblical allusion to the seven-holed human skull. When this bowl is "broken," physical death ensues, and "the spirit shall return unto God who gave it."[150]

HOW PRAYERS ARE ANSWERED

The National Center for Complementary and Alternative Medicine in the U.S. defined prayer as an active process of communication and appeal to a higher spiritual power. In every culture and religion prayer is the most common method of connecting with and appealing to the divine. Compared to other spiritual practices, such as yoga, meditation, and transcendental meditation, prayer is far more popular, not only among Americans, but also among people who live in India. According to a Pew Research Center survey, 55% Americans say that they pray every day, 23% pray weekly or monthly, and only 21% said they never pray. God also grants our prayers. According to one study, 70% of people who pray reported that prayers are very helpful.[151] Intercessory prayer means that someone or a group of people pray on behalf of another person, most commonly for health and well being. Harding reported that intercessory prayers do in fact have a healing effect.[152]

There are several theories on how prayers work.

Studies have shown that prayer gives an ill person hope for recovery, and positive emotions act through a mechanism called the mind-body connection. However, more recently scientists are exploring another mechanism by which prayers are answered. According to this hypothesis, prayer acts as a channel for supernatural intervention. Faith is an important aspect of prayer. However, God is the only entity in the

---

149. Matthew 27:33.
150. Ecclesiastes 12:6-7. For more on this topic, see Lochlainn Seabrook. *Jesus and the Law of Attraction.* Sea Raven Press, 2014, pp. 51,188, 211, 388, 390, 491, 517-518.
151. McCaffrey AM, Eisenberg DM, Legedza AT et al. "Prayer for health concern: results of a national survey on prevalence and pattern of use." Arch Intern Med 2004; 164:858-862.
152. Hardings OG. "The healing power of intercessory prayer." West Indian Med 2001; 50:269-272.

universe who has the power to choose whether or not to answer a petitionary prayer. When God grants a prayer, it acts through a mechanism that transcends any naturalistic mechanism known to us.[153]

Quantum entanglement is a phenomenon that was described by Einstein as "spooky action at a distance." In quantum entanglement two subatomic particles separated by a distance can act in a similar fashion, as if they are connected, and can communicate with one another. This is very similar to the concept of telepathy, in which two individuals are separated but can mentally communicate with one another. Although this phenomenon is rarely found among humans, at the subatomic level it is not uncommon. Knowing that subatomic particles are the building blocks of the universe, one can loosely interpret that quantum entanglement is a phenomenon that connects everything within the universe; thus we are all linked: God, you, and me, just as Jesus declared.[154]

Leder commented that the human mind is non-local in nature (not confined to the physical brain), and during distant healing a healer can be connected to the person requiring healing through some mechanism related to quantum entanglement. Similar mechanisms may explain telepathy and other psi phenomena.[155]

The concept of quantum entanglement can also be interpreted as a possible mechanism of how a praying person can be connected to God, sending him a petition for help. If we are all connected then we are indeed also connected to God, because although he is beyond space and time (and the fabric of our universe), he created the universe and knows how to interact with his creation. Therefore, God must hear all our prayers, and depending on our petition, decides whether he wishes to answer our prayers or not.

Two years ago one of my closest friends lost his job and I prayed for him. A job then appeared from nowhere and the salary was higher than his previous job. He also prayed and his other friends prayed for

---

[153]. Jantos M, Kiat H. "Prayer as medicine: how much we have learned?" Medical J Australia 2007; 186:S51-S53.
[154]. John 14:20. For more on this topic, see Lochlainn Seabrook. *Christ Is All and In All*. Sea Raven Press, 2015, passim.
[155]. Leder D. "Spooky action at distance: physics, psi, and distant healing." J Altern Complement Med 2005; 11:923-930.

him as well. This prayer was answered too. However, this year I prayed to get a national award. I did not get it. But in the annual meeting when they announced the winner, I understood why. The recipient of the award was far more qualified than me.

SOUL AND SUPREME-LORD (SUPERSOUL)

In the Rig-Veda the human soul is referred as the *atma* and the Supreme Lord as Brahman. But both the *atma* and the Supreme Lord are connected to each other. In the Upanishads the human soul is referred to as *Jiva-Atma* (a Sanskrit word meaning "individual soul") and the Supreme Lord as *Param-Atma* (a Sanskrit word meaning "supersoul").

This concept is also found in the Bhagavad-Gita, where it is stated that besides our physical body, we have another transcendental entity representing the supersoul, which oversees our actions and attempts to guide us in the right direction. Therefore, every human soul is divine in nature, which is precisely what Jesus stated,[156] and it is our goal to get connected with the supersoul at the end of our physical existence.

There is a story in the Upanishads about two friendly birds who are sitting on the same tree. One bird (the soul) is eating fruits, while the other bird (the supersoul) is watching his friend, but living in a transcendental state, and not interested in the material world. The bird eating the fruits is enjoying material pleasures, but also faces all of the anxieties and other negative emotions inherent to the material plane. The other bird is completely detached from material pleasures, and in the process avoids the pain of the material world. This bird is in a state of eternal joy, one that transcends physical pain and pleasure. If the fruit-eating bird would only follow the example of the other bird (the supersoul), all of his stress would disappear. For then the fruit-eating bird would become one with God.

ASTRAL PLANES: WHAT HAPPENS WHEN WE DIE?

According to Hindu scripture, when earthly lessons are learned and karma reaches a point where spiritual progress is no longer possible

---

[156]. John 10:34. For more on the topic of theosis, or "God in Man," see Lochlainn Seabrook. *Christ Is All and In All*. Sea Raven Press, 2015, passim.

on earth, it is time for the soul to journey to another realm. Death is referred to as *mahaprasthana*, in Sanskrit meaning a "great journey." Death is part of a natural process, similar to the fall of ripe fruit from a tree.

Our individual soul (*atma*) is immortal, for there is no weapon that can destroy a soul, fire cannot burn a soul, ice cannot freeze a soul, water cannot dissolve a soul, time cannot degrade a soul. It is eternally pristine, fresh, sinless, birthless, and deathless. It truly is, as the writer of the book of Hebrews commented, "without father, without mother, without descent, having neither beginning of days, nor end of life."[157]

Therefore, "death" is not really death as it is thought of in the traditional manner (the "*end* of life"). It is actually the *beginning* of a new phase of life. For when the soul leaves the physical body it is like discarding an old suit of clothes. The soul is then "born again" into another dimension or parallel universe (heaven).[158]

According to Hindu scriptures each soul has five layers: the physical body (Sanskrit, *Sthula Sarira*) is the first or outer layer. The second layer is the etheric body (*Linga Sarira*), which is an exact duplicate of the physical body. The inner-layer is the astral body, which contains the mental body and the casual body. The innermost layer of the astral body, the casual body (*Karan Sarira*), contains the fabric of the soul. The seven Chakras are situated in the etheric body. The astral body is connected to the physical body with a cord (the biblical "silver cord"),[159] which is severed at physical death so that the soul can be set loose from the body.

After the cutting of the silver cord, the etheric body leaves the physical body, and in case of violent death or if the soul is not developed, the soul may roam on the earth plane and appear as a ghost. This in-between spirit world is known as "limbo" in Christianity, and as *pretaloka* in Hinduism. A departed person with an etheric body may continue to believe that he/she is still physically alive for up to several days, and then a spirit guide from a higher realm must step in to help the confused soul.

---

157. Hebrews 7:3.
158. John 3:3; 1 Peter 1:23.
159. Ecclesiastes 12:6-7. For more on this topic, see Lochlainn Seabrook. *Jesus and the Law of Attraction*. Sea Raven Press, 2014, p. 352.

However, if the physical body is destroyed, then the departed soul is no longer confused. This is the reason Hindus cremate dead bodies. At this point, the departed soul sheds his/her etheric body, and continues to exist in an astral body, which, as mentioned, is an exact duplicate of the physical body.

This Hindu deity is an androgyne named Ardhanarishvara. Half man (on its right) and half woman (on its left), it represents the inseparable unity of the Male and Female Principles. Christianity has its own androgyne, the *Elohim* of Genesis, a double-bodied god-goddess. Hence the Bible declares that during the creation of the universe: "*Elohim* said, 'Let *us* make man in *our* image, after *our* likeness.'" Despite the suppression of the truth about this verse by mainstream Christianity, the writer of Genesis puts it plainly: "So *Elohim* created man in his own image, in the image of *Elohim* created he him; *male and female* created he them."

It is important to note that the soul has no gender: a male can reincarnate as a female and vice versa. However, during life in the astral plane the astral body resembles the physical body before death, but has more senses than the five senses of the physical body. When a human soul exists as an astral body, this body is an exact duplicate of a younger version of the physical body (when the person was 20-35 years old).

There are seven planes. Our earth being the lowest one is made of atoms and molecules (lower vibration). There are six more planes above earth which are made up of finer subatomic particles (finer vibrations) compared to atoms and molecules, which are the building blocks of earth and the visible universe. The higher the planes, the higher the vibrations. Accordingly, as one progresses upward the landscapes change from wonderful to spectacularly magnificent, and eventually to a level of supreme beauty that is beyond description. Moreover, each layer of the higher planes may also have up to seven sub-planes.

After death some souls with only their astral body go to the first astral plane above earth (this is the second level, because the earth plane or material world is considered the first plane) to purge earthly desires from their astral bodies. Therefore, the second level is a type of "purgatory," as described by Catholics, which washes away sin and prepares the soul for its journey to the next level.

Someone who was materialistic or shallow on earth may spend more time at this level compared to someone who lived a more exemplary (spiritual) life. Staying on this plane for an extended period of time may be painful because a soul may still retain its human desires; but there is no way to fulfil these kind of desires on this plane. For example, if a soul loves to control others as he did while living on earth, this desire is impossible to fulfil in the astral plane because there is no one else to control. Moreover, if a person has unfulfilled sexual desires while living on earth a soul may feel these same strong urges while living on the astral plane, but with no way to fulfil them. However, one spiritual teacher told me that astral sex is possible in the second plane, but this might delay the progress of a soul.

There are lower planes than earth, places that are unsightly, drab, and even horrible, where evil people go after death. God is not angry with those who are exiled here. It is merely time for them to acknowledge their bad karma and to understand how their malicious inhumane actions hurt other people when they were living on earth.

According to Hinduism there are seven layers of hell, with the lowest and worst layer intended for people who committed horrible crimes against humanity. However, no soul remains permanently in hell—unless they choose not to continue their spiritual growth. The sooner they repent of their evil deeds, the sooner they can move to a higher plane; otherwise they must reincarnate into a difficult life situation on earth in order to pay for their sins.

My spiritual teacher in India told me that seeing someone suffering in this world does not automatically mean that he/she committed evil acts in a past life. Sometimes a child born with a birth defect must suffer in this world in order to burn residual karma, so that the soul can break away from the cycle of birth and death, and be with God all the time (which in Sanskrit is called *mukti*). Sometimes a poor man who does not have enough food to eat while on earth may choose to select a hard life in order to burn his/her residual karma from a past life. This allows him to achieve total freedom from the cycle of birth and death. Therefore, we should not judge others. Only God knows why someone is having an arduous earthly life.[160]

Most souls (good people) transit to the third plane through the second plane, but some souls may go to the third plane directly if they have lived laudable lives while on earth. In the third astral plane, although the astral body retains the gender of the physical person, there is no gender. The astral body is indestructible and does not require any food or sleep. Moreover, the astral body never gets sick.

This level of the astral plane is called "Summerland" by Western theosophists. Summerland is significantly more beautiful than earth, but has earth-like mountains, lakes, rivers, and oceans, and life there is very enjoyable. While living in this plane a soul can meet deceased relatives and friends, as well as feel the blessings of God.

Other celestial beings also live on this plane. These beings, although non-human, may look like humans but are very attractive. Female celestial beings are called *Apsaras* in Sanskrit, while male beings are called *Gandharva*, and are usually engaged in singing or playing musical instruments.

Angels often visit this plane. Here, souls can travel freely as if they are flying. Moreover, all the knowledge of the universe is available, and a curious soul can learn the mysteries of the universe in an instant. Therefore heaven starts at the third plane.

My spiritual teacher Deepak Babu told me that a soul living on the third plane may voluntarily decide to go back to earth because the earth is a school. Therefore, making spiritual progress on earth is much faster than on an astral plane. In this case a soul, along with a spiritual guide, decides whether to be born rich or poor, male or female, Asian, European, or African, genius or mediocre, etc., all depending on a mutually agreed lesson plan for making the maximum spiritual progress during the upcoming reincarnation. However, due to their evil deeds, those souls living on the lower planes may not have any choice.

My spiritual teacher Deepak Babu also told me that souls living

---

160. Matthew 7:1.

on the third plane (and above) can create anything they want using their imagination. For example, if a couple had a magical time visiting a tropical paradise while living on earth, and enjoyed a spectacular sunset on the Pacific Ocean while sitting at their cottage, they can recreate that magical moment on the astral plane using their imagination. Then the sunset can last as long as they wish. He also told me that our universe is full of many alien lifeforms from various alien planets. Some planets are inferior to the earth, while other planets are far superior.

Our earth is unique: there is enough spiritual light so that a human being can make enormous spiritual progress here in order to be united with God after death. However, on planets superior to earth most people live very spiritual lives, crime, lust, and racism are unknown, and negative words like "hate" do not exist in their languages.

Interestingly, each alien planet with life also has unique astral planes specific to that planet. Although most earthbound souls will reincarnate on earth again until they break away from the cycles of birth and death, under special circumstances, based on the judgement of high level masters who are in direct communication with God, an earthbound soul may reincarnate onto a highly evolved alien planet. Moreover, with the help of a spiritual guide a soul who wants to see God's creation, not only on earth, but on alien planets, may be given permission by God to travel anywhere, exceeding the speed of light to appreciate the many different lifeforms elsewhere in the universe.

A soul may remain in the third level (lower heaven) and may make enough progress to go to the fourth level (higher heaven). More spiritually advanced souls transit to the fifth plane. Most likely at this stage a soul will shed its astral body, retaining only its mental and casual bodies. Highly evolved human souls, as well as gods, goddesses, and angels, live on this plane. Going beyond the fifth plane is quite difficult, as one needs to live his/her life engaged in selfless acts while achieving tremendous spiritual progress. Level sixth is reserved for highly evolved souls who have divine knowledge while living on earth.

The highest level, the seventh, is extremely difficult to reach. Here, a soul sheds its mental body and keeps only its casual body (*Karan Sarira*). This is God's personal world and anyone living on this plane is in constant communication with the Supreme Lord, and has the ability to go anywhere in the universe or any other universes, and is not constrained by space and time. Although there is no negative emotion beyond the third astral plane, the seventh astral plane is constantly illuminated by God's consciousness. It is 100 percent positive and pure. There are planes above the seventh astral plane. But these are God's regions and so not much is known about them.

Interestingly, anyone living on the fourth plane or beyond can transit to a lower plane, including hell, to help someone. But no one living on the third plane can go to the fourth plane, unless accompanied by a spiritual guide. Therefore, if a wife is living on the fourth plane, she can visit her husband living on the third plane at will, but her husband cannot go to the fourth plane to see his wife. (Various astral planes described in Hindu scriptures are summarized in Table 3.) Highly evolved spiritual masters living on the fifth and sixth planes, however, can travel anywhere whenever they like. Jesus lives in heaven with God, which I believe is beyond the seventh astral plane. But he can go to any plane, even hell, to help a disturbed soul sincerely in need.

To the enlightened this illustration of an Indian statue of Buddha is identical to Christian depictions of Jesus, beginning with the fire coming from the Crown Chakra at the top of Buddha's head. Christian artists give Jesus a halo or nimbus, the Western version of Buddha's flame. In both religions these symbolize the same thing: self-realization or atonement (that is, at-one-ment) with God. As in Buddhism, Jesus taught the doctrine of the Third Eye (shown here at the center of Buddha's forehead), saying: "The light of the body is the eye: if therefore thine eye be single, thy whole body shall be full of light." Divine Inner Light, or *en-light-enment*, that is.

While we live on earth we are bound by the laws of the country we live in. Similarly there are rules that we must obey while living on any one of the many astral planes. All astral planes, including the earth, are under God's control; but starting with the third astral plane the presence of God is felt all the time, because, as noted, heaven begins here. Since we do not have earthly desires while living on these higher astral planes following the rules will come naturally to us.

While living on earth no one can read our minds. I can dislike someone but not express it openly, and no one will ever know. That individual might even think I like him. On the higher astral planes, however, we do not talk verbally, but communicate telepathically. On the other hand, we cannot hide our emotions from others. If a soul can transit to the fourth level, they may have broken the cycle of birth and earth. Any soul living on the fifth or sixth levels is free from reincarnation, but at God's desire he/she may decide to be reborn on earth in order to help humanity. God also sent his own son Jesus for our salvation.

ASTRAL PLANES: IS THERE ANY SCIENTIFIC PROOF?

There is no scientific proof that astral planes exist. Similarly, the concept of parallel universes and higher dimensions are speculations based on scientific theories, such as quantum mechanics and string theory. However, science has limitations. Therefore, where science ends philosophy begins, and where philosophy ends spirituality/religion begins. No experiment can be conducted to either prove or disprove the existence of God. Therefore, faith is important.

In the Bhagavad Gita three paths are described for attaining God realization:

1. Understanding God through knowledge (*Jnana Yoga*).
2. Understanding God through selfless work (*Karma Yoga*).
3. Understanding God through faith and devotion (*Bhakti Yoga*).

However, the path of devotion (total faith) is the most desirable and probably the easiest way to connect with God and feel his divine love at all times.

Although not scientifically valid, an interesting approach is to consider that astral planes exist as or in parallel universes. Since gravity can leak through the fabric of our universe to a parallel universe, the human soul may have the same capacity. Parallel universes may not follow the same space and time concept that our universe does, and time there may move both backward and forward.

Another possibility is that astral planes or heavens represent higher dimensions, and these higher dimensions are not visible to the naked eye. God is beyond space and time, but he created the natural laws of space and time. Therefore, he can do anything and appear anywhere instantaneously, and most likely prefers to take a luminous human form when he does.

WHY GOD TOLERATES SATAN

Since God is the ultimate power he must have created Satan. Indeed, according to the Bible God created all "darkness" and all "evil."[161] But why? Why would a loving God allow human suffering, natural disasters, crime, and terrorism? Why did God allow Hitler, Stalin, Mussolini and other wicked world leaders to brutally murder so many innocent people? He is all powerful and if he wanted to he could have easily prevented them from committing genocide. While God is pure consciousness and positive emotion, Satan represents negative consciousness and evil. There are many good books on this topic in which religious scholars explain why God allows evil acts. One such book is written by Timothy Keller.[162] In this section I am only going to describe what my spiritual teachers in India taught me.

God is omnipotent. Therefore, God can destroy Satan anytime at will. However, without night we cannot appreciate daylight, without sorrow we have no concept of joy. This creation manifests a playful side of God (Sanskrit, *Leela*), one with no beginning and no end. Therefore, in living our lives we are playing a cosmic game with God; but we are not aware of this due to the illusion or veil of *maya*.

The Supreme God is playing hide and seek with us due to his playful nature. As soon as the veil of *maya* is lifted and we understand that this is just a game, there is no need to involve our emotions. When we play the game for the game's sake, we break away from the cycle of birth and death. Therefore, there is no success or failure in life when we look at the bigger picture. A multimillionaire and a penniless person will both die one day and both will face the same God.

The question then is, should we stop working because there is

---

161. See Isaiah 45:7.
162. Timothy Keller. *Walking With God Through Pain and Suffering.* Dutton, 2013.

no need to earn money, take care of family members, raise children, etc.? Nearly 2,000 years ago Paul was faced with this same question, when some of his followers at Thessalonica stopped working because they believed that worldly things did not matter anymore. Paul reproached the group, commanding them to return to work and "stand fast" in the Lord.[163]

Indeed, we should remain firm in our faith and think about God day and night. My teachers told me that God wants us to play with him. Therefore, we each have many purposes in life. We need to go to school, graduate, get a job, raise children, and enjoy life. But at the end of each day we must think about God and our mortality.

There is nothing wrong with being materially successful, being a millionaire or billionaire, making earth-shattering discoveries, winning a Nobel Prize. But one should remember that his or her achievements are only possible because God wants the person to be successful. Money should be looked upon as God's money, and after taking care of all one's material needs and living a comfortable life, the extra money should be spent in helping others who are not as fortunate. Many affluent people have foundations through which money is used for charitable causes. This makes God happy. God does not tolerate pride. Being humble is a noble quality.

Although God loves to play cosmic games with us, he also wants us to love him and connect with him rather than indulge in earthly pleasures. Sorrow is our wakeup call. But pain is our teacher.[164] When we face hurdles in life we look to God and understand our true purpose. Moreover, in a battle between God and Satan God always wins, even if it does not seem like it at the time.

Hitler killed millions of people and almost occupied half of the world. But in the end the Nazis surrendered to the Allied forces and Hitler committed suicide at a bunker in Berlin. Osama Bin Laden orchestrated the horrific destruction of the World Trade Center, murdering thousands of innocents. But he himself was finally killed by the courageous agents of the American Special Forces.

If we look at history, evil forces are always defeated by good

---

163. 2 Thessalonians 2:15; 3:10-12.
164. Lochlainn Seabrook. *Jesus and the Law of Attraction*. Sea Raven Press, 2014, p. 324.

people who belong to the army of God against Satan. In real life sometimes I see good people suffer while bad people thrive. My very religious friend who lives an exemplary life lost his only son in 2013 and does not understand why God did this. However, what surprises me is that despite this terrible loss, he still loves God.

There are many things in this world I do not understand. It is better to be humble and accept the fact that I know nothing.

DOES JESUS LOVE EVERYONE OR ONLY CHRISTIANS?

As I discussed in the first chapter, I went to a missionary school when I was a child and as a result, Jesus is close to my heart. When I was in Chicago a group of people tried hard to convert me to a particular denomination of Christianity. They were persistent and came to my apartment every Saturday between 9 and 10 AM. They wanted to convince me that only Christians (their particular denomination of Christianity) are allowed to go to heaven and everyone else will go to hades and will burn in hellfire for eternity.

Jesus inviting Peter to walk on the water to meet him. The Apostle began to sink. Not because it was impossible, but because he allowed fear to overrun his faith. Catching him by the hand, Jesus said: "O thou of little faith, wherefore didst thou doubt?" As Amitava's wife Alice proved, it is not faith in science, but faith in the Unseen Imperishable God that works miracles in our lives.

I politely told them that I believe in Jesus, but I do not want to be converted because I am very comfortable being a Hindu. Moreover, as a Hindu I can still love Jesus because there is no conflict. They disagreed and continued to show up every Saturday morning. After two months I asked them what happened to all the human beings who had died before Jesus was born. It should not be their fault that they had no chance to accept Jesus as their savior. Are these souls burning in hell even today? They had no answer and eventually left me alone.

My wife Alice is a Christian and she accepts Jesus as her savior. She attends church regularly on Sunday mornings and never forces me to go with her. I go to church with her when I wish. My mother, who is a devout Hindu, never even asked Alice to convert to Hinduism. Similarly neither my wife nor her parents ever asked me to convert to Christianity.

There is only one God and all paths eventually lead to God. As food nourishes our body, religion nourishes our soul and helps us to connect with the divine. As an Indian I prefer butter chicken masala to baked chicken; but my American wife prefers baked chicken to butter chicken masala. However, both foods serve the same purpose.

Similarly, I like to pray in Sanskrit and my wife likes to pray in English (she does not know Sanskrit and I have never tried to teach it to her; it is unnecessary to know Sanskrit to find God). But the same God listens to both of us.

When I visit Kolkata I always go to a historic church in Bandel situated by the River Ganges, because I can feel the presence of Jesus there. I believe Jesus loves everybody who trusts his divine power and accepts him as their savior. After death, if Satan wants to possess my soul and drag me to hell, I will beg Jesus for help, and I am confident that he will rescue me—despite knowing that I am a Hindu.

DO GREAT SCIENTISTS BELIEVE IN GOD?

Many great scientists including Nobel Laureates have faith in God. Isaac Newton said, "What we know is a drop, what we do not know is a vast ocean. The admirable arrangement and harmony of the universe could only have come from the plan of an omniscient and omnipotent Being." Alessandro Volta, who discovered the basic principles of electricity (after him electrical measurement is still often expressed as "volts"), said, "I confess the holy, apostolic and Roman Catholic faith. I thank God who has given me this faith, in which I have firm intention to live."

Charles Darwin, who discovered the theory of evolution, said, "I have never denied the existence of God. I think the theory of evolution is fully compatible with faith in God. I think the greatest argument for the existence of God is the impossibility of demonstrating and understanding that the immense universe, sublime above all measure, and man were the result of chance."

Albert Einstein, the founder of modern physics, said, "Everyone who is seriously committed to the cultivation of science becomes convinced that in all the laws of the universe is manifest a spirit vastly superior to man, and to which we with our powers must feel humble." Erwin Schrödinger, who discovered wave function (the fundamental basis of quantum mechanics), said, "The finest masterpiece is the one made by God, according to the principles of quantum mechanics."[165]

WHERE CAN I SEE GOD?

The true nature of God is beyond human perception, but throughout this book I have tried to convince you that scientific evidence suggests that human consciousness lives beyond physical death, and that the information gathered during one's lifetime is not lost when the physical body dies. Extensive research indicates that many features of NDEs, for instance, cannot be explained by our knowledge of neurobiology. Thus I believe it is safe to say that during an NDE people are actually visiting an unearthly realm, one we call "heaven."

Being a scientist does not mean that a person has to be an atheist. Science is far from knowing everything, and there are certainly other realms (such as parallel universes) that are not visible to us, and which cannot be detected by even our most sophisticated instruments. Therefore, there must be a God. God comprehension is well beyond my intellectual ability. I cannot realize God using my head, but I can feel his presence in my heart.

God loves us and that is the reason the world is so beautiful, with snow-capped mountains, great sweeping plains, vast oceans, and dense forests, as well enormous deserts, such as the Sahara and the Gobi. Our earth is full of incredible flora and fauna. I do not need to travel thousands of miles to see oceans and mountains, because I can enjoy the beauty of a spring dew drop on a rosebud right in my backyard.

My spiritual teachers told me that the glory of God is like seeing the illumination of millions of suns. The human eye cannot bear the full glory of God. Therefore, he can take any form that makes his follower happy.

---

165. *Religion*, June 26, 2014: 25. "Famous scientists on God." www.aleteia.org/en/religion/article/25-famous-scientists-who-believed-in-god-58831. Accessed July 2, 2015.

As I have said, my mother is a devotee of Lord Shiva, and so she sees God as Lord Shiva. The modern day sage Ramakrishna talked to the Goddess Kali in the Dakshineswar temple (in Kolkata) as if she were a living being. Some claim to have met and spoken with the flesh and blood Jesus, said to still visit earth on occasion to aid humanity in its ongoing spiritual growth.

But God manifests in an infinite number of other ways as well. There are compelling reports of credible people seeing goddess-like figures in the ruins of ancient civilizations; luminous fairies dancing in circles in the midst of dark woods; long "extinct" dinosaurs living in dense forgotten jungles; and mermaids sunning themselves on the beaches of isolated coves. And we should not neglect to mention the thousands of sightings of the Loch Ness Monster, Bigfoot, extraterrestrials, thunderbirds, ghosts, and scores of other bizarre creatures and strange phenomena not recognized by mainstream science. How do we explain these things?

It is not possible for my cat Thor to read the morning newspaper. Similarly, it is beyond me to understand the Supreme Being. However, I see the faces of God every day in wild flowers, a spectacular sunset, a crystal clear blue sky after rain, in the loving face of a mother, the generous face of a father, and the kindness of everyone around me. I feel the love of God through the love of my wife, my parents, my in-laws, my close friends, family members, and even sometimes from strangers who help me for no reason.

Swami Vivekananda asked: "Why do you search for God when he is before you in many forms?" Look at his creation and feel his presence everyday. If you want to serve God, help fellow human beings selflessly. Anyone who helps a fellow human being is serving God.

CONCLUSIONS

God lives in the heart of every human being and God is everywhere. Scientific evidence clearly reveals that there is another realm which cannot be studied scientifically, and that the human soul is almost certainly real and survives the death of the physical body. Therefore, there must be a God who lives beyond science and who created everything; yet being omnipresent, he is with us all the time. Believers know these things to be absolutely true and do not need science to "prove it." For like Paul they "walk by faith, not by sight."[166]

The best way to live is to be happy with life, and instead of seeing the glass half-empty see it as being half-full. I always count my blessings and thank God for what I have instead of focusing on what I cannot achieve due to my limitations. There are many times when I get frustrated because I do not get certain things. But later I realize that this is because I have not yet spiritually earned them.

If I consider earthly life a cosmic game, then I want to win it by playing by God's rules, not by cheating my fellow players. In the end I want to be able to go home happily knowing that my father God will welcome me and forgive me for the sins I committed unknowingly during my play.

Amitava and his wife Alice at the Great Wall of China in 2002.

---

166. 2 Corinthians 5:7.

TABLE 1
SUPREME GOD AND TRIMURTI (HINDU TRINITY)

NAME	COMMENT
Brahman	Supreme God, the only eternal entity, who is pure consciousness, existence, and bliss, as well as absolute, impersonal, changeless, eternal, and all-pervading.
Brahma	Brahma the "Creator" is not eternal and lives for 100 Brahma years, which is the equivalent of 311 trillion 40 billion human years. After that time he will die and the entire universe will be destroyed. Then the supreme God Brahman will create a new Brahma who will be in charge of creating a new universe. Brahma lives under the constraints of space and time that govern our universe.
Vishnu	Vishnu, also known as Hari or Narayana, is the "Preserver." Vishnu does not die when Brahma dies, but during the destruction of the universe everything enters into Vishnu, giving him gigantic form, one known as Maha Vishnu. Everything inside Maha Vishnu will be in an unconscious state until the birth of a new universe.
Shiva	Shiva is the "Destroyer," but there are many other interpretations. He probably lives beyond space and time as there is no mention of his death in Hindu scripture.

TABLE 2
NAME OF VARIOUS CHAKRAS AND THEIR FUNCTIONS

WESTERN NAME	SANSKRIT NAME	LOCATION	COLOR	COMMENTS
1st - Base Chakra or Root Chakra	Muladhara	Base of spine (tailbone area)	Red	Basic needs for survival, feeling of being grounded
2nd - Sacral Chakra	Svadhishthana	2 inches below naval (pelvis area)	Orange	Well-being, material pleasure, sexuality
3rd - Solar Plexus Chakra	Manipura	Upper abdomen	Yellow	Self-confidence, thinking, and intellectual abilities
4th - Heart Chakra	Anahata	Center of the chest	Green	Relationship, love, compassion, forgiveness
5th - Throat Chakra	Vishuddha	Throat region	Blue	Communication, trust, expression of feelings
6th - Third Eye Chakra	Ajna	Between eyes	Indigo	Decision making ability, wisdom, intuition, psychic ability
7th - Crown Chakra	Sahasrara	Top of head	Purple	Spirituality, connection to the Divine

TABLE 3
VARIOUS ASTRAL PLANES DESCRIBED IN HINDU SCRIPTURE

LEVEL OF PLANES	SANSKRIT NAME	COMMENTS
1st Plane	Bhuloka	Earth, the lowest plane; where we live.
2nd Plane	Bhurvarlok	This plane above earth is where the soul sheds all earthy desires before moving to higher levels. This level is probably the same as the Catholic "Purgatory."
3rd Plane	Swargoloka	Lower heaven, often called "Summerland" by Western theosophists. Beginning here landscapes become significantly more beautiful than on earth. The temperature is perfect and souls live in peace and harmony and often feel the presence of angels and God.
4th Plane	Mararloka	Middle heaven, which is significantly more beautiful than the 3rd plane. Here inhabitants feel the presence of God and angels all the time.
5th Plane	Janaloka	A higher heaven where many Hindu gods and goddess (also angels) live.
6th Plane	Tapoloka	A very high plane where only the most spiritually evolved souls go. Souls reaching this level do not reincarnate, except under special circumstances, e.g., if God requests that they go back to earth for mass education/spiritual progress.
7th Plane	Satyaloka	The highest plane, beyond good and evil. If a soul attains this level, it is perfectly united with God. It is difficult to comprehend this plane. Planes higher than the 7th may exist, but nothing much is known about them.

MEET THE AUTHOR

AMITAVA DASGUPTA was born in Calcutta (now Kolkata), India, in a Hindu family and from his childhood on had a keen interest in science, philosophy, and religion.

He was lucky to meet gifted spiritual teachers in India and also later in the U.S., but he was a "doubting Thomas" because science cannot explain the nature of God. However, in 2011, when his mother came back from death after the prayers of his Christian wife, he became a believer.

In the U.S. he received his Ph.D. in chemistry from Stanford University and his Fellowship training from the Department of Laboratory Medicine at the University of Washington School of Medicine at Seattle.

Dr. Dasgupta lives in Houston, Texas, with his wife Alice and two cats named Thor and Minnie. He has published over 20 books, mostly on his professional field, toxicology. This is his first attempt to write a spiritual book, sharing with readers his life's journey from a skeptic to a believer.

MEET THE COAUTHOR

LOCHLAINN SEABROOK is an award-winning author, Bible authority, and Civil War scholar. The most prolific and popular Southern historian and writer in the world today, he is known as the "new Joseph Campbell" for his numerous work in the fields of comparative religion and mythology, as well as theology and thealogy.

He is a recipient of the prestigious Jefferson Davis Historical Gold Medal and the author of over 45 books whose topics range from Jesus, the Bible, and ancient Goddess-worship, to American history, social issues, and family histories.

A seventh-generation Kentuckian of Appalachian heritage and the sixth great-grandson of the Earl of Oxford, Mr. Seabrook has a forty-year background in biblical exegesis, hermeneutics, and higher and lower criticism, the paranormal, American history, Southern history, and is the author of the worldwide bestseller, *Jesus and the Law of Attraction*.

If you enjoyed this book you will be interested in these related titles from Sea Raven Press:

- CHRIST IS ALL AND IN ALL: REDISCOVERING YOUR DIVINE NATURE & THE KINGDOM WITHIN
- JESUS & THE LAW OF ATTRACTION: THE BIBLE-BASED GUIDE
- CHRISTMAS BEFORE CHRISTIANITY: HOW THE BIRTHDAY OF THE "SUN" BECAME THE BIRTHDAY OF THE "SON"
- JESUS & THE GOSPEL OF Q: CHRIST'S PRE-CHRISTIAN TEACHINGS AS RECORDED IN THE NEW TESTAMENT

Available from Sea Raven Press and wherever fine books are sold

ALL OF OUR BOOK COVERS ARE AVAILABLE AS 11" X 17" POSTERS, SUITABLE FOR FRAMING.

SeaRavenPress.com

www.ingramcontent.com/pod-product-compliance
Lightning Source LLC
Chambersburg PA
CBHW031258110426
42743CB00040B/728